Let's Stop Playing Games

Let's Stop Playing Games

Finding Freedom in Authentic Relationships

JOE LINEBERRY

WITH FOREWORD BY GARY CHAPMAN

RESOURCE *Publications* • Eugene, Oregon

LET'S STOP PLAYING GAMES
Finding Freedom in Authentic Relationships

Copyright © 2011 Joe Lineberry. All rights reserved. Except for brief quotations in critical publications or reviews, no part of this book may be reproduced in any manner without prior written permission from the publisher. Write: Permissions, Wipf and Stock Publishers, 199 W. 8th Ave., Suite 3, Eugene, OR 97401.

Resource Publications
An Imprint of Wipf and Stock Publishers
199 W. 8th Ave., Suite 3
Eugene, OR 97401
www.wipfandstock.com

ISBN 13: 978-1-61097-481-3

Manufactured in the U.S.A.

Unless otherwise noted, Scripture quotations are taken from the NEW AMERICAN STANDARD BIBLE®, Copyright © 1960, 1962, 1963, 1968, 1971, 1972, 1973, 1975, 1977, 1995 by The Lockman Foundation. Used by permission.

Scripture quotations marked MSG are taken from *The Message* by Eugene H. Peterson, Copyright © 1993, 1994, 1995, 1996, 2000. Used by permission of NavPress Publishing Group. All rights reserved. www.navpress.com (1-800-366-7788).

Scripture quotations marked NIV are taken from the Holy Bible: New International Version © 1973, 1978, 1984 by International Bible Society. Used by permission of Zondervan Publishing House. All rights reserved.

To Beth, my dear lifesaver and loving mentor

Contents

Foreword ix
Acknowledgments xi
Introduction—Why Read This Book xiii

SECTION ONE   THE GAMES

- Chapter 1   ESP Games 3
- Chapter 2   Don't Change Me Games 12
- Chapter 3   Avoiding Responsibility Games 24
- Chapter 4   Isolation Games 37
- Chapter 5   Be Perfect Like Me Games 53
- Chapter 6   Passive Be Like Me Games 67
- Chapter 7   Serve Me Games 83
- Chapter 8   Looking Good Games 92

SECTION TWO   THE GAME CHANGER: LETTING GO OF THE OUTCOME

- Chapter 9   Imagining a Life Without Our Games 105
- Chapter 10   Letting Go: Steps 1 and 2: Relieving the Pressure 112
- Chapter 11   Letting Go: Steps 3 and 4: Experiencing the Freedom 124

SECTION THREE   WHERE IS GOD IN ALL THIS?

- Chapter 12   God's Work as the Ultimate Game Changer 139
- Chapter 13   Living Authentically with God 150
- Chapter 14   Where Are You, God? 156

Bibliography 161

Foreword

RELATIONSHIPS ARE NOT NEARLY as easy as they seem. Just look at the evidence. A large percentage of marriages end in divorce, a number of adult children are estranged from their parents, and countless employees leave their jobs because they "can't get along" with a co-worker or a supervisor.

In my years of counseling, I noticed that we naturally blame the other person when a relationship is strained. We then move on to other relationships, but in time we discover that relational problems follow us wherever we go. In spite of this evidence, we fail to see that our behavior has contributed to the problems in our relationships. Unfortunately, we are not good judges of our own emotions and thought patterns, and how they affect our behavior.

We are all unique in our responses to life. My way of thinking may be very different from yours. The emotions I feel may seem unwarranted to you, but my emotions and thoughts actually guide my behavior. Since I am often unaware of my emotions and my thought patterns, I simply behave in a way that seems logical to me. We end up doing what we consider to be perfectly normal, but what other people may consider to be abnormal or inconsiderate.

None of us wants to end up lonely and isolated from others. Instead we long for warm, supportive, encouraging relationships. Rather than protecting these important relationships, we subconsciously act to protect ourselves. We end up hurting others and sabotaging our relationships. These subconscious responses fall into certain defensive patterns. Joe Lineberry describes them as "games we play." Unless we understand these patterns and develop more loving responses, we will miss out on the joys of authentic living.

This book offers practical help in identifying the common "games we play," why we play these games, and how to develop new patterns of behavior that produce better relationships. Such relationships do not simply happen. They require insight, the willingness to change, and positive action. This book is designed to guide you on the path toward healthy relationships.

Gary Chapman, author of *The Five Love Languages*

Acknowledgments

I DON'T MEAN FOR this to sound like I have won a Gospel Music Award, but I cannot avoid giving credit to God for this book. Many of the ideas in this book came out of "thin air," often in the middle of the night. At times the book seemed to write itself. When I started writing about these games two years ago, all I had in mind was to record our family's relationship games and list some ways to help us stop playing these games. I am amazed at how purposeful the book now appears, setting out a vision of authentic relationships and a possible path to become authentic lovers. I confidently say that these ideas are not my own. Writing this book has been a way of journaling my conversations with God—I think I hear him most clearly when I am writing. Thank you, Lord.

I also thank the writers who have already documented their ideas and their relationships with God and others. You can see that I have been strongly influenced by Gary Chapman's God-inspired, practical advice and by Larry Crabb's journey with God.

I especially thank my wife, Beth, for her insights and her willingness to be open about our relationship—the good, the bad, and the ugly. I am grateful for her patience with my writing at odd hours (night and day), taking away from our quality time together. Of course, I suggest that our times together are now better as I have personally tried to stop playing my games and apply these game changers to our life with each other.

I thank our sons (Steve, Brent, and David) for being an integral part of our stories in this book. I regret that they experienced the brunt of some of my games, and yet I am glad that they experienced some transformation through my brokenness. I am also grateful to my sons and our daughters-in-law (Erica and Megan) for reviewing several stages of the book and offering their suggestions.

I thank my friends for providing examples of the games we play and the game changers which transform us. In particular, I want to acknowledge the time and effort of many friends who encouraged me with their ideas and moral support, including Bill and Cindy Ketner, Jim and ENan Baldwin, Debbie Barr, Chuck and Lucretia Pruett, Neal Millsaps, and Terri Vaughan. I really appreciate the input from my men's group (Mike Dixon, Rodney Hughes, and John Vestal) for taking six months to test how the book works as a group study, even while the book kept changing as a work in progress. You "anal-ytical" readers can thank these guys for the tables and summaries in the book. I am also indebted to many friends who have shared their games and stories with me, helping me understand how they struggle to be authentic (of course, their names have been changed to protect the innocent). Thanks also to Jane Kelly for formatting the original layout, Mike Key for copyediting the final manuscript, and Chuck Westbrook for adding his professional insights.

I am grateful to Lifeway Press for permission to quote excerpts from the Beth Moore video series, *Esther: It's Tough Being a Woman*. I also appreciate Christian Amondson and his team at Wipf and Stock—their patience and their willingness to work with an author like me, who has no obvious fan base. Finally, I am thankful for Jonathan Wilson-Hartgrove's compassionate help in navigating the world of publishing and his introduction of Wipf and Stock.

I look forward to the insights to come from you who read *Let's Stop Playing Games*. As you share your stories, your games, and your game changers, we will all grow to become more authentic lovers of God and each other.

Introduction

Why Read This Book

As an only child, I grew up playing lots of games by myself. My love for games evolved into creating my own games—board games, sports games, and even crossword puzzles. I have always enjoyed games, especially the ones that I was good at—the ones I had a chance to win. The games allowed me to succeed in an imaginary world, where I could avoid my real-life issues and win my share of the games.

Over the years I noticed that my wife, Beth, the rest of our family, and I played games in our relationships—crippling games that kept us from addressing the real issues at hand. They weren't obviously manipulative or wrong—they were subtle. Of course, I wanted to win my fair share of these relationship games, too. My problem was I couldn't think as quickly as Beth, so I lost most of our arguments. So I came up with another strategy. I started naming these games. Once I named one of Beth's games, I had a better chance of offsetting her advantage in that situation. Of course, it was easier to see the games Beth played than to see or admit the games I played. Fortunately, Beth was kind enough to help me see my games, too.

So it hit me. If identifying these games takes away their power and allows us to address the real issues in a loving way, why not let others in on this secret? Once the mystery of these games is unveiled, we can choose to interact with each other in more loving and honest ways. We can be transformed into an authentic, loving community where we no longer need to play these games. Wouldn't that be a great place to live!

So let's get to the bottom line on how I believe this book can help you and me. Here is my hope: Applying these game lessons will improve and even heal our relationships by:

- exposing our unhealthy relationship games and why we play them;
- replacing our games with more loving ways to live, thus allowing us to develop a lifestyle of authentic living;
- creating an open and fun atmosphere for discussions with our friends and family—we are all in this together.

> **READING HINTS**
>
> This book is intended to be an interactive book. I don't claim to know all the answers. (At least I don't want to look like I think I know all the answers. Is that a Looking Good Game?)
>
> The observations and conclusions of this book are drawn from the experiences of my family and friends. I may have left something out that you think is critically important. You may also disagree with one or more of my observations or suggestions. That's great! Apply these ideas to fit your own personality and culture. Make this your book.
>
> Since it is designed to be interactive, I suggest that you read the book while pretending that I am there with you. We are discussing these ideas and suggestions, interacting with each other, sharing our stories. At the end of each chapter, reflect on my observations and suggestions—are they true for you? How might you apply these concepts in your life? What would your life look like if you or others didn't play these games?
>
> Hopefully, it is a "fun" read, which will encourage you to read the book with a family member or a set of friends. Interact with each other, share your stories and apply these concepts with each other. You don't have to fully agree with me or even with each other when you discuss these ideas. As you share honestly with each other and try to apply these suggestions to your lives, you'll start living a more loving and authentic life.
>
> If you want to take our pretend interaction to a more realistic level, visit me at http://discuss.exploringpossibilities.net. I would love to hear from you!

Before we start exposing our relationship games, let's delve into the recesses of our minds for a moment. What's going on inside our subconscious when even the best of us sabotage our relationships?

I'm not sure about what you're thinking, but here's what is going on inside me. I know that leading a loving life is actually in my best interest. My life will be the most rewarding if I don't look out for myself but instead give myself in loving others—being kind, patient, forgiving, courteous, humble, generous, and honest.[1] It seems that God has placed in each of us a heartfelt desire for intimacy—to love and to be loved. Developing loving relationships with others helps fulfill that inner desire for authentic relationships. I want to love others daily, moment by moment, decision by decision, person by person—that is my stated, number one goal.

So I get it. I know caring for others is best, but I often choose otherwise. In spite of my desire to practice love as a way of life, my natural tendency is to maximize my comfort or fun and to minimize my pain. "Will this be fun?" is often a key factor in my decision whether to do something. (It's scary to think that could be my life goal—it sure doesn't feel or sound loving.) I am not doing anything bad, just trying to have some (deserved?) fun and avoid pain. In any case, I carry out my "increase fun/reduce pain" goal by planning my life and orchestrating events and/or people so I end up enjoying life or medicating my pain, most of the time. Some people might say I am controlling or manipulating events and/or people—"planning" sounds more acceptable.

> **OUR NATIONAL MOTTO**
>
> By the way, I don't think I'm alone. Maximizing our comfort and reducing our pain appear to be a national pastime. In many cases, it is all about me. I miss the bigger picture, that something beyond me is ultimately important and worth sacrificing my comfort. I focus on myself. My goal is: How can my life be more fun?
>
> Or maybe your story goes like this. At one time you trusted in God, but you endured some great pain or sadness. You may have repressed the memory, but the pain and sadness linger. In your view, God didn't protect you from that pain then, so you can't trust him now. You are afraid of what else might happen to you. You

---

1. Chapman, *Love as a Way of Life*, xxii, 5.

> have to take things into your own hands—it's up to you to protect yourself from pain.
>
> I could argue that this is our real national motto. How would this look on our coins? Instead of "In God We Trust," our coins could be inscribed with "More Comfort/Less Pain." It might appeal to those who just want more fun in their lives, as well as those who are medicating their pain. Either goal, it's up to me to achieve it. Oh, but I digress. Or do I?

I become self-focused when my comfort is threatened, especially if I anticipate something painful is coming. At that point, loving others is secondary. My basic human survival instinct kicks in and I feel the need to protect myself—most often trying to protect myself from emotional pain or even emotional death. In that moment, protecting me against the fear and pain of the situation becomes more important than any potential reward of loving others.

Larry Crabb has similar explanations for why we avoid authentic relationships—shame and fear:

> Shame. Shame is powerful. It can be life controlling. At all costs, I feel compelled to protect myself from ridicule, rejection, or revulsion. Facing the worst about me in the presence of someone who matters to me is unbearably painful. It's personal suicide, the end of self-respect, of any confidence that I could be loved. . . . [For example] three women get together. One displays her conversational competence. She listens well and asks good questions. Another, when the conversation turns serious, hides her fear of appearing shallow behind deflecting humor. The third tells painful stories as though she were reciting facts. She doesn't want to feel her pain. She wants to come across as a "together" woman. All three are subtly addicted to the approval they passionately fear losing. Their fear guides the way they relate.[2]

In my civilized, Christian tradition, I act like these three women. With fear guiding my decisions, I have a hard time admitting that I am not acting authentically or in a loving way. I may not even notice, because it is so natural to protect myself from my discomfort, pain, and fears. So I hide my intentions from myself. I play manipulative "games"—pro-

---

2. Crabb, *Real Church*, 44, 89.

tecting myself and addressing my fears without realizing or admitting it. I am no longer acting out of love. And I see others playing the same relationship games. These games are crippling our relationships—not just our family, not just our friends, but really all relationships suffer with these games.

I have noticed a pattern about these games. I found that once I identify a specific game, it is easier to overcome the temptation to protect myself the next time that I am in the same situation. It's easier to turn it around and act out of faith and love, not out of fear. In this book, I have identified eight types of relationship games as a way to jumpstart the process of purging these games from our lives.

You may also find it easier to see the games your spouse or best friend (or even best enemy) plays than to see the games you play to protect yourself. We need each other—what a loving way to live, where we ask each other to bring to light the games we have been playing. Then you and I have a better chance to admit our fears and games, and even better, we are now free to make a loving decision.

> **WHAT IS A GAME?**[3]
>
> In this book I define a "game" as a self-protecting process we go through to deal with our fears or possible pain. Typically, it is a

---

3. I am not the first writer to refer to manipulative actions in our relationships as "games." Many writers refer to flirting, playing hard to get, etc., as natural and effective dating games. These games supposedly add a touch of mystery and romanticism to our one-on-one, intimate relationships. The logic here is to not be too transparent, because if the other person really knew your intentions (marriage, a one-night stand, etc.), he or she might be turned off. Where does mystery stop and deception/lying begin? While this book does not specifically address these types of dating games, this topic of transparency in dating relationships would be a great topic for discussion with your friends and family.

Eric Berne wrote *Games People Play—The Basic Handbook of Transactional Analysis* in 1964. His use of the term "game" sounds similar to my definition. For example, Berne defines a "game" as "an ongoing series of complementary ulterior transactions progressing to a well-defined, predictable outcome [a payoff] . . . . Every game is basically dishonest." (p. 45) I think that's similar to my definition of "game" as a manipulative, inauthentic way to protect myself against some perceived threat in a relationship. Berne would probably argue that there are many motives in play with these different games, and he has a well-developed formula for applying Transactional Analysis concepts (for example, Parent, Child, Adult ego states) to help people improve their relationships.

To the extent I understand Berne and his associates, it appears we are addressing similar games from a different world view. While they see life through a Transactional Analysis lens, I see life through God's calling for us to be reconciled, loving, and authen-

self-focused process that keeps us from being loving and authentic in our relationships. Usually the game involves some form of hypocrisy or manipulation of others. Instead of accepting and patiently loving others, we evaluate and judge them. We even judge ourselves. Throughout the book I refer to people who play these games as "gamers."

Let's also address what is not a game:

- A game does not include our obvious attitudes or acts of evil—murder, lying, stealing, arrogance, envy, hatred, betrayal, etc. When we act or intend to act in these ways, we are clearly not embracing love as a way of life. Even if we rationalize our attitudes or actions, we know we are intentionally harming others. When we play games, we often have many of these same evil attitudes of arrogance, selfishness, etc. We just try to keep our manipulative, selfish behaviors from being so obviously evil.

- Sometimes self-protection is very appropriate and not tied to gamesmanship. For example, if you are an emotionally or physically battered person in a relationship, you are *not* playing a game when you try to confront your abuser or escape that toxic environment. You demonstrate your love for that person when you hold the abuser accountable for his or her cruel actions. If you don't respect yourself enough to protect yourself in this situation, you will probably enable your abuser to mistreat others in the future. In contrast to this appropriate self-protection, we tend to play games when we try to protect our pride or our self-focused desires.

By the way, our goal is not to become so focused on our games that identifying them is now our passion. Ignoring other people while calling ourselves on our games is just another way to play a game and avoid caring about others. The idea is to stop playing the games so we are free to love others.

---

tic in our relationships. Therefore, our proposed solutions to stop playing these games are different. Hopefully, the loving solutions and game changers offered in *Let's Stop Playing Games* are helpful to you.

WHAT'S NEXT?

Now it's time to review the games—see if you can find yourself in any of them. They are all found in section 1 of this book. To help organize these relationship games, I have put them into the following categories:

- Don't Change Me Games—games that justify our refusal to be more loving

- Avoiding Responsibility Games—games where we blame others so we cannot be held accountable for our decisions

- Isolation Games—games where we isolate ourselves and shut others out of our lives

- Be Perfect Like Me Games—games that push others to act and think like we do

- Passive Be Like Me Games—more subtle games, where we judge others and sometimes manipulate them to act like we do

- Looking Good Games—games designed to make us appear to be better (for example, more considerate or more popular) than we really are

- ESP Games—a substitute for actual communication and interaction with others, where we speculate about other people's motives

- Serve Me Games—games where we manipulate others to do what we want them to do, which ultimately benefits us

Then in section 2 we will review an important game changer, an attitude adjustment that helps us stop playing these games. With this game changer, we can turn this vision of authentic and loving relationships into a lifestyle of trusting relationships.

For those who are interested, we will wrap up with section 3, Where Is God in All This? That seems to be a fitting question since we are trying to be more loving, and I believe God is the author and creator of love. So what is God's role in improving our relationships?

So I say, "No more delay! Let the games begin!"

Our "Crippling" Games

There is an easy way to remember these games. The first letter of a key word in each type of game actually spells the word "CRIPPLES." If we don't do anything about these games, they will cripple our relationships.

I admit I feel embarrassed to use something hokey like this, especially the line, "If we don't do anything about these games, they will cripple our relationships." Talk about working hard to make this "CRIPPLES" idea fit the theme of the book.

As embarrassed as I feel, at the same time it does give my brain a "hook" to remember the games. For those who think this is helpful, this memory hook looks like this:

Don't **C**hange Me Games
Avoiding **R**esponsibility Games
Isolation Games
Be **P**erfect Like Me Games
Passive Be Like Me Games
Looking Good Games
Esp Games
Serve Me Games

I don't know if you noticed, but I just pulled off a Looking Good Game. If you think this memory hook is helpful, I gave it to you. If you think it is hokey, I just agreed with you. I am playing both sides of the fence, trying to look good to each group. I never really committed to you about my real feelings—hopefully each group of readers will think I am on your side.

Section One

The Games

1

ESP Games

I am concerned that you will take advantage of me, so I protect myself by guessing your motives and intentions (with an ESP Game). Instead of playing this game, I will take the time to listen to you, ask you questions, and seek to understand you.

Jon and Laketia love to to go to the mall or sit in an airport and observe people as they walk by. They then make up stories about these strangers—what is going on in their lives at this moment in time. Some people call this "people watching." I call this the ESP Game, because Jon and Laketia are acting as if they have Extra Sensory Perception (ESP), which allows them to clearly see what is going on in the lives of these strangers. For example:

> Jon: See that couple over there—the guy with the blue suit and the woman behind him with red shoes. He's the one with a big scowl on his face. They're really hustling down the airport concourse—almost running.
>
> Laketia: The woman with him—I bet that's his wife—she doesn't look happy, either. What a grim face! And she's jogging at least ten feet behind him, and losing ground. I can't believe she can jog like that in those heels.
>
> Jon: They sure look like they've just had an argument. I bet he thinks she made them late.
>
> Laketia: He's got that businessman look. Probably they're going on a business trip to New York City, and she's coming along for a fun weekend with him.

Jon: Not starting out as much fun right now, is it? Look, he's calling someone on his cell phone—probably his admin assistant to see if she can hold the airplane at the gate. Just like a businessman to think the airline should respond to his beck and call.

Laketia: Nah. He has no hope for that to happen. [*pauses*] His wife might as well turn around and go back home if they miss this flight. The weekend won't be worth his constant criticism of her.

This ESP Game seems like a harmless game for Jon and Laketia to play, as they enjoy some downtime together. Look at how many assumptions they made about this couple. Then look how successive speculations are built on previous parts of the story, as if they knew their previous assumptions were correct. While Jon and Laketia would joke that they are confident in their ESP story, they know that their speculations are probably way off base, and their stories become less accurate as they build on their previous assumptions.

Virtually all of us play ESP Games with our real relationships. Since the ESP Games are often the foundation for playing our other games, I have reviewed them first. In these games we guess what is going on in other people's lives, just like Jon and Laketia are doing at the airport. The problem with the ESP Games is that we play them in real life and then act as if our speculations were true.

I have identified one major ESP Game that we play a lot, probably at least once per day (maybe once every hour or so). I call this game the "What Are They Up To?" Game. When we don't trust other people, even including those close to us, we want to know "what they are up to."

PLAYING THE "WHAT ARE THEY UP TO?" GAME

In the "What Are They Up To?" Game, we are trying to figure out the motives and intentions of other people. We don't necessarily know what others are thinking or feeling, and we don't trust them to tell us the truth. So we guess. Of course we have past experiences with our friends, family, and co-workers. We combine those experiences with our ESP and we become very confident that we know their motives and intentions.

We don't just speculate about their motives—for some reason we typically assume the worst motives as we play this game. Then we proceed to act on that assumption, as if it is true. For example:

- My restaurant manager tells me that whatever specials I want to create for dinner will be fine. The more creative, the better. I wonder, "Does she really mean this? She is the pastry cook—what if I create a new pastry item for the day? Can I really stray that far from what the executive chef has cooked before?" So then I act on that assumption and don't create any new pastry items. I don't even create any new specials.

- I arrive home and Beth meets me with "Why are you coming home so late?" I assume she is mad and that I am in trouble. So I react defensively and an argument ensues.

- My teenage son doesn't come home at curfew and he is not answering his cell phone. Based on my past experiences with my son, I speculate that he has been in a wreck, or he turned off his cell phone to avoid talking to me, or once again he is not respecting our house rules and me. When he walks in the door thirty minutes late, I yell, "Why are you coming home so late?" and then proceed with a lecture about responsibility before he can even answer my question.

One other thought: If you are like me, you will now notice how often you speculate about other people's lives—their thoughts, their intentions, what is behind their successes and problems. It's pervasive—I think I guess what someone else is thinking or feeling several times a day. I picture this invasive vine (kudzu, for you Southerners, is a good example) curling around the trunk of a tree, so intermingled among the limbs and leaves that it is hard to distinguish the vine from the tree. That is how entangled our lives are with these ESP Games. I speculate, therefore, I am. It is so natural. Not necessarily loving, but natural.

WHERE DO WE FEEL THREATENED? HOW DO WE TRY TO PROTECT OURSELVES WITH THESE GAMES?

I speculate that we speculate in the ESP Games to overcome our fears of the unknown. We are trying to control our lives to ensure our success while limiting our problems. We don't really know what is going through someone's mind or heart, yet we feel we need to know, so we can maximize our comfort and protect ourselves against possible pain. In the above ESP Game examples, I appear to be protecting myself against the fear of failure (will my cooking be acceptable?), the fear of disappointing my wife, or a wide range of fears regarding my teenage son (from death to disrespect). I don't really know if these fears are real, but I strongly suspect they are real as I play the ESP Games.

If the other person tells us his motives, logically that would take away our need to play the "What Are They Up To?" Game. Yet we still feel we have to play that game, because we don't even trust what he is saying or doing. Our culture teaches us to be skeptical of everything we read or hear. Is anyone telling us the whole truth? We don't think so. Surely they are acting out of some hidden self-interest and not looking out for our welfare. We feel the need to protect ourselves against their hidden agendas. We guess what the other person is really wanting and then work off that speculation to decide whether to meet his "real request." Otherwise, we risk losing money, getting laughed at, looking stupid, etc., if we believe them and let them take advantage of us. And if we let our skepticism get the best of us, we avoid committing to anyone or any cause. No one can be trusted.

> **SPECULATING ABOUT WHY WE SPECULATE**
>
> Reader (that's you): You know, I caught you. You are playing an ESP Game when you are speculating about our fears as we play these ESP Games. You tried to be sneaky and use the word "speculate." The ESP Games and "speculation"—they're the same thing. How do you rationalize playing an ESP Game to analyze the ESP Games?
>
> Joe (that's me): You're good, you know that. My speculation or analysis is based on personal experiences of my friends, my family, and me. I am not trying to convince you that my observations or experiences apply to everyone. Instead, I see that this book is more about me sharing my observations (= speculations) about these games we play and you examining your life to see where these observations strike a chord with you. I actually hope you figure out other games you are playing, which I haven't even thought of. Once you do that, you have a better chance of eliminating these games from your life and then be free to love, freed from fear and shame.

WHAT ARE THE UNINTENDED MESSAGES WE ARE SENDING?

When I am guessing another person's motives, I am sending at least one of three messages:

- I don't care enough about her to spend more time trying to understand her or what is really going on in her life.
- I won't trust her even if she explains more about her feelings and intentions.
- Trying to protect myself is more important than helping her.

Practically, the person I am speculating about probably doesn't even know I am speculating about her, so how does she get these messages? Obviously, one of my confidants could tell her what I had guessed about her. Or, I could give away my distrust with my body language or my tone when dealing with her. Otherwise, without some other communication or action on my part, the "speculatee" (is that a word?) probably only gets the message that I am ignoring this issue in her life.

But what about the message I am sending to you, my friend and confidant, when I share my speculations about someone else. I bet you eventually personalize my speculations and think I will guess your motives, too. If I speculate about someone else's motives or troubles, then logically won't I do the same to you (either within my mind or behind your back)? Can you really believe I won't eventually treat you the same way—not trusting you or caring about you?

WHAT ARE SOME LOVING SOLUTIONS TO REPLACE THESE GAMES?

One of the challenges with the ESP Games is that we often don't even know our own motives or intentions. Since that is true, how well do you think we can guess someone else's motives? Or how well can we know all the aspects of another person's life? We don't really know all that is going on.

Second, we base most of our assumptions on our past experiences. While past experiences and patterns of living provide a reliable basis for our assumptions, they are not 100 percent accurate. We may keep the other person stuck, not allowing him to actually change.

Finally, our speculations are affected by our own past and our dreams for the future, as well as what is going on in our own lives now. We cannot step out of our own story and objectively assess what is going on in other people's lives. Our observations and speculations are filtered by our brains—they are not objective.

Besides these logical reasons to consider a more loving solution, I have to recognize that playing this game feels emotionally safer than trying some other strategy. The obvious alternative is to take the time to listen to the other person, seeking to understand her thoughts and feelings, maybe even seeing if I can help her. If I try to explore the issue further, I risk:

- not liking the pain involved with what else she has to say;
- the time involved to work through an issue with her;
- having to decide whether to believe her—now it could be obvious I don't trust her.

If safety and comfort are my goals, it's easier to just reject her with partial information than to deal with rejecting her after hearing more from her. If I change my mind later, I can just blame my earlier distrust on not knowing the full story—just a simple misunderstanding. Thus, I don't have to admit I was wrong.

For introverts and conflict-avoiders like me, taking the time to listen to another person is a real challenge, especially since guessing what they are up to can be done so easily. I have found reflective listening to provide a good way to listen, when I make the conscious effort to use this tool. In the above situations, I could use reflective listening to help me communicate rather than trying to guess what is going on. For example:

- Cook: [*to the restaurant manager*] When you say I have complete freedom to develop any specials I want to, I get concerned that I may overstep my bounds. I really love to try creative dishes, so what type foods should I stay away from? I know the executive chef developed some creative dishes—did any of his creations not work for some reason?
- Joe: [*to Beth*] Sounds like you're angry that I am late.
- Father: [*to teenage son, whenever they get to talk again*] "I feel disappointed and angry when you miss your curfew and don't call to

explain what is going on. It makes me think you don't really care about me or our family. Any thoughts?"

One way to make this work is to put your fear into words and then state your fear or concern to the other person. I have actually found the process of vocalizing my fears is a freeing experience. No need to speculate when I state what I am speculating about. Then I just wait for the other person to respond. I can still decide whether to trust his answer. At least now I have gotten my ESP-driven concern out in the open.

Notice how each person vocalizes his hidden concerns or fears in the above examples:

- Cook: [*to the restaurant manager. The cook was afraid he would go too far, so he just vocalizes his fear*] I get concerned that I may overstep my bounds.

- Joe: [*to Beth. I am afraid she is mad at me for being late, so I just state my fear*] Sounds like you're angry that I am late.

- Father: [*to teenage son, whenever they get to talk again. The dad is afraid his son is rebelling and just rejecting him, so he includes this statement*] It makes me think you don't really care about me or our family.

When I take the time to think through what is scaring me about a specific situation, I have found this process of stating my concerns to be relatively easy.

One of my managers at work used to give this advice if we thought a co-worker had treated us wrongly or was trying to take advantage of us: "Give'em the benefit of the doubt; then go and check it out." Go directly to that person and verify what you heard. This is sound advice to avoid playing the "What Are They Up To?" Game. It's really a simple solution—either take the time and effort to state your fears and confront the issue (person) in a loving way, or don't bother speculating at all. If it is worth speculating about, it is worth risking the opportunity to find out the truth.

WHAT ARE SOME POSITIVE ASPECTS OF THESE GAMES?

Empathizing with others is a loving way to understand what other people are going through. It is critical to developing authentic relationships. With empathy we are in a better place to help and care for another person. We can use aspects of these ESP Games to try to empathize. "If I were in her situation, how would I feel and what would I want to do?" is a place to start.

Of course, speculating with good intentions does not mean that you will correctly guess how that person is feeling. If possible, the more loving option would be to talk to the person. You could say, "If I were in your situation, I would probably feel angry and would want to quit." Then see how the other person responds. Don't ask, "Is that how you feel, too?" Give the other person the freedom to not tell you how he is feeling or what he wants to do.

You could also use reflective listening. "It sounds like you are angry and may just want to quit." Once again, make the statement about your observation, and don't follow up with a question to verify your speculation. Try not to put the other person on the spot. Let him respond to your statement as he sees fit.

Notice that in these examples I have speculated about feelings and possible actions. I have not guessed motives. I think speculating about another person's motives should be done with great caution. I don't know my own motives, and to speculate about or even ask someone his possible motives is rarely helpful. When some issue arises, I usually guess that the other person has self-centered, "out-to-get-me" motives. What is he up to? What is he trying to do that could hurt me? (Maybe I am just assuming that person has the same selfish motives or intentions I would have if I were in his shoes.)

If you think your intentions are loving, you could ask, "Would you be interested in exploring why you acted this way/why this has happened in your life?" Just be prepared for the other person to say "No." If "No" is the answer, then let it go.

One other thought: It can be helpful to explore your own motives. "What led me to feel or act this way?" However, don't let this self-reflection consume you. If it absorbs your time, you are wasting too much time focusing on yourself, when you could be loving others. Ask God to help you know your motives and see what comes to your mind. Then move on, trusting that he has revealed to you what you needed to know right now.

SO HOW ABOUT YOU?

1. What stories do you have like these? In other words, what ESP Games do you see other people playing (either ones listed in this chapter or others you can think of)? What ESP Games do you play?

2. How often do you speculate about others' motives and then act on your speculation?

    a. Rarely

    b. Once per week

    c. Once per day

    d. Several times per day

3. What would life look like if you didn't play ESP Games?

2

Don't Change Me Games

I am afraid of the uncertainty and possible pain of changing, so I protect myself by refusing to improve myself (with a Don't Change Me Game). Instead of playing this game, I will recognize change is inevitable and ask God what to change and how to change.

Over the years Beth and I have tried to help our friends when they have encountered marital problems. Some of our married friends have subsequently gone through the pain of divorce. Beth and I typically become despondent in these situations, wanting to hug each other and not let go. We question if we could become divorced and unable to reconcile our differences, since it is happening to our friends. We actually play a type of ESP Game, trying to figure out their motives and intentions and mistakes, so we don't repeat them in our marriage.

One consistent pattern we have seen in many of these divorcing couples is that at least one of the spouses is not willing to change. That spouse refuses to go to marriage counseling. Or the couple does go to counseling, but that spouse is not willing to change his/her lifestyle for the sake of his/her mate or the marriage. It appears to me that the uncooperative spouse is playing a Don't Change Me Game.

You don't have to have marital problems to play these games. A couple of Don't Change Me Games (I'm sure there are others) are:

- "This Is Just the Way I Am" Game
- Going on the Defensive Game

Both games give me permission to not try to change. I am basically saying, "The status quo is as good as it is going to get. Take it or leave it."

PLAYING THE "THIS IS JUST THE WAY I AM" GAME

Think about the times you have said, "This is just the way I am." You may have already said it to yourself as you read the last chapter. Perhaps you felt pressured to change some habit or attitude that you really didn't want to change or feel able to change. Sometime during the conversation you may also have said, "I'm trying as hard as I can. I just can't do anymore."

If you are like me, sometimes you actually could change, but you just don't think it is important enough to try. For example:

> Beth (that's my wife—you probably remember that): I wish you would organize your papers in the study. They are an unsightly mess.
>
> Joe (that's me—you probably remember that, too): You know that I get no satisfaction out of organizing my stuff. It feels like such a waste of time. Then I can't find anything. I am more comfortable with my piles.
>
> Beth: Your piles don't need to be out when our friends come over. I will feel embarrassed about the mess. Why do you think I am cleaning up my stuff?
>
> Joe: Our friends know me and accept my junky piles. They surely won't be surprised, and I won't feel embarrassed. You know this is just the way I am. I will just close the door to the study.

This verbal exchange could easily be resolved if I was willing to just straighten up my papers. Obviously, I must have some other plans that I think are more important, so I just hide behind "this is just the way I am" without disclosing what I am really planning to do with my time.

I have also played this same game regarding my introverted personality. When it comes to being an introvert, it really is harder to change. Even if I act differently (outside my introverted comfort zone), I am still by nature introverted. I still prefer interacting with one or two other people, rather than trying to communicate within a large group of people, especially a large group of people I don't know. A large crowd saps my energy. I usually feel my conversations within a large group are so superficial (probably my way of coping is to keep the conversations superficial). So a conversation with Beth might go like this:

> Beth: Tom is headed to Afghanistan, and I was thinking Laura and I could get all our neighbors together to send him off with our best wishes.

Joe: That sounds like a nice thing to do for him, but you know I don't like large groups. Can't we just have Tom and his wife over for dinner or something?

Beth: Don't you think you could survive this party? You know most of our neighbors enough to talk to them. An evening of superficial conversations won't kill you. Besides, you're the one who decides to make them superficial. (Beth knows me too well.)

Joe: I am just an introvert and this is just the way I am.

Beth: If this were a work-related function, you would figure out a way to survive. You only play the introvert card if it isn't related to work. I think work is all you care about.

Joe: Sounds like you are going on the offensive to me. This must be really important to you to have this party. (Wow! Would I say this and not get defensive? Maybe this book really is helpful.)

Beth: Well, to be honest, Laura and I have already picked a weekend to have the party.

I really can't change my personality. Of course, I can choose to support the party and deal with my personality discomfort. As Beth said, I really will survive, and this is a way to show Tom and his family we care about the hardship they are going through. We could end up compromising on the type of party, so that the group isn't so large. Or, I could make a point to try to get to know one or two other neighbors, rather than trying to "work the crowd." Several choices—I am not really as hemmed in as I first felt.

I actually can throw in a comparison and take the "This Is Just the Way I Am" Game to a more advanced level. I don't just tell you that I am not planning to change, but I also show you that you should be grateful that I am as good as I am. Why even consider changing? I am not as bad as Jimmy (substitute your favorite comparison person here), who is a lot worse than me. In other words, you have unrealistic expectations of me. "Give me some credit" is going through the back of my mind, perhaps followed by "just give me a break and get off my back."

Let's pick back up on my discussion with Beth, where I was determined to not clean up my papers, and see how I can elevate the discussion by comparing myself to someone who is worse than I am:

Beth: I wish you would organize your papers in the study. They are an unsightly mess.

Joe: You think this is a mess. You should see your cousin's office during tax season. I don't see how he gets anyone's tax returns right with all that mess. Just be glad my piles are confined to one corner of the study.

I improve my chance of success at this game if I pick someone that Beth would agree is worse than I am. It is actually counter-productive to compare myself to someone that Beth actually admires. If Beth doesn't share my judgment of the other person (her cousin, in this example), it just adds fuel to our disagreement.

> **OUR ILLOGICAL SOLUTIONS TO OUR PROBLEMS**
>
> One of my fellow consultants was griping about getting a speeding ticket at a certain town in Virginia. Our conversation went something like this:
>
> Bart: I can't believe I got another speeding ticket going to see this client! I get one every year.
>
> Joe: You do what? Get a ticket in the same town each year? And you always get it going to see the same client?
>
> Bart: Yeah. It really hacks me off!
>
> Joe: Wow! What are you going to do to stop getting these speeding tickets? (At this point, I felt like this was a leading question, leading Bart to agree to an obviously logical answer to stop speeding, at least to stop speeding when he drives through that Virginia town.)
>
> Bart: I've thought about that, too. I'm going to get me one of those Fuzzbusters. I'll know when there's a cop nearby so I won't get caught speeding again.
>
> Joe: [*laughing at the irony of the situation*] Gee! I thought you would just stop speeding.
>
> Bart: Nah! Why would I do that?
>
> It's so funny how we rationalize a solution to our problem that continues to feed our problem. Bart won't stop speeding, but he will go to the expense and trouble to buy a Fuzzbuster. I wonder—what keeps us rationalizing our Don't Change Me Games instead of just trying to address the real underlying problems in our relationships?

PLAYING THE GOING ON THE DEFENSIVE GAME

Going on the defensive is a common Don't Change Me Game. We go on the defensive and somehow justify our actions or our decisions, especially if someone is trying to get us to change the way we act in the future. All of us are especially good at recognizing when someone else is playing this game. Our response is so automatic and simple, "Don't be so defensive." So what are they saying that tells us they are being defensive? Let's make a list of the responses that show us that our friend is going on the defensive. Maybe when these same words come out of our mouths, we can notice and stop ourselves before we go on the defensive. For example:

"That's just not true."

"You don't know what you're talking about."

"You don't really understand (me or my motives)."

"You don't really understand (everything going on in this situation)."

"I wouldn't have acted that way if . . ."

"_____" (you fill in the blank)

Now let's add these responses at the end of a possible conversation between a manager and an employee at work—during the employee's annual performance evaluation and planning session. You know—the discussion you have to have with your manager before he tells you if you are getting a pay raise, and if so, how much the raise will be. Or perhaps the discussion that precedes getting put on probation for your work performance, which is the final step before you are fired. Of course, your manager always wants to talk about where you can improve during the next year. You can feel the tension already—elevated heart beat, sweaty palms, and so on.

> Manager: I compared your self-evaluation on your performance review to my scores for your work this year. We have discussed the areas where we agreed. Now let's discuss areas where I think you can improve over the next year.
>
> Employee: [*thinking "Here it comes now," and dreading where this is headed—takes a deep breath*] Okay.
>
> Manager: I saw that you gave yourself "Exceeds Expectations" for the category "Communicates Effectively." I put that down as an area

that "Needs Improvement." So let's talk about how you can improve your communications with your supervisor.

Employee: [*already thinking defensively*] Give me some examples where I fell short. I think I'm a very organized person who communicates well with everyone.

Manager: One example is that issue with Jane at ABC Company. Remember how you got their information late and did not communicate to your supervisor that you were going to be late with your work. We were not able to reassign some of your work until the project was already late. At the time, we talked about letting your supervisor know ahead of time if you are running into a problem with a deadline.

Employee: That's not exactly how it happened [= *That's just not true/ You don't know what you are talking about*].

Or

Employee: You don't really understand. I was trying my best [= *My motives were good. I can't improve*].

Or

Employee: You don't really understand everything that was going on at the time.

Or

Employee: As you recall, I wouldn't have been late with this project if the client had gotten me their data on time, and if I hadn't been so tied up on other projects.

Or

Employee: _____ (substitute your defensive response)

I would say this employee is not open to trying to improve, wouldn't you? He's more interested in defending himself.

By the way, we don't need to be in a work situation to go on the defensive (as if you didn't know that). For example, I think the response, "You just don't understand me," is one you wouldn't typically use at work, but it gets a lot of use in my personal confrontations. Also, "I wouldn't act this way if this had not happened/if you hadn't done this to me" is a common defensive reaction in all parts of our lives.

WHERE DO WE FEEL THREATENED? HOW DO WE TRY TO PROTECT OURSELVES WITH THESE GAMES?

Change is inevitable. Nothing is certain. Everywhere you turn, you see reminders of this fact. We see images on television and in our theaters (both news and drama and even comedies) that reinforce the message. Some of our political leaders promote change as the way to a better life, while other politicians warn us of the dire consequences of the proposed changes—the solution will be worse than the problem ever was. We also see this play out in our own lives and in our friends' lives. Change occurs and we feel so out of control. We feel threatened to the core.

I think that's it! When I play a Don't Change Me Game, I am trying to exert more control over my world. I don't really want other people telling me what to do or how to live. I perceive their suggestions as even more than criticism, more like an infringement on my life—another area I cannot control. I seem to be afraid of what I will lose if I try to change. Known pain is better than unknown gain, especially if I don't see anything to gain from changing. Or maybe I do see something to gain, but the change will require more energy than I have right now. I want to scream out, "I can only do so much! Give me some breathing room here."

I also play these games when I prefer to deny some issue in my life, rather than deal with it. I throw out one of the Don't Change Me Games as a defense mechanism. Some issues have no easy answers, so I just don't deal with them at all. Changing has too many unknowns—it's foggy out there. The fallacy in this logic is "not changing" has a lot of unknowns, too—for some reason I don't see the foggy unknowns of not changing as easily as I am scared of the fog of changing. I think if I don't change, that I am somehow in more control of my life. It just feels safer.

> ### GET SOME SLEEP
>
> It is now 4:00 a.m. in the morning. I woke up around 3:00 a.m. after having a nightmare. My mind was racing and my adrenaline was flowing, trying to correct some client problem that I had messed up in my dream. It wasn't real, but tell my body that now.
>
> In a few hours Beth will ask me why I couldn't sleep, why I left the bedroom to come downstairs. She will probably be concerned, because I have awakened in the middle of the night for three of the last six nights. Looks like a pattern, especially when I am typically a sound sleeper. Maybe it is a pattern—I don't know.

> She will express her concern, and I will be tempted to play a Don't Change Me Game or an Isolation Game (coming soon to a chapter near you). In other words, either I will slough it off and not want to talk about it (Isolation Game), or I will get defensive because I guess she would want me to try to get some help, from a physician or someone like that (Don't Change Me Game).
>
> I am confident there is no easy answer. It's not exactly like I can now tell my body, "Get some sleep!" and it will automatically respond. I can speculate for hours on possible causes—getting older, some unknown illness, taking on too much responsibility at work, not trusting God, etc. Each one of these possible causes carries some possible change in my life, and each change seems so full of the unknown. I can even downplay this issue further by pointing out friends who are currently dealing with much more life-threatening or family meltdown issues than my recent sleep issue. I really have it easy. No wonder I want to just go on the defensive and deny this could be a problem.
>
> It's not that I don't want to change; I don't even know what to change. Actually, I don't want to change, either. And of course, I would only want to change whatever is causing my sleep issue. Why change anything else, if it isn't causing a problem?
>
> We all deal with areas like this, where this is no easy answer, where we are tempted to jump into a Don't Change Me Game. When I see all these ongoing problems and I run out of strategies, I finally ask God for help, not just for me but now for all these other people and their issues. Even helping my friends deal with their issues requires changes from me.
>
> God, what are you doing in my life and my friends' lives? What do you want me to do? How do you want me to be? As scary as this request is, how do you want to *change me*? Oh, help me to trust you with my fear of the foggy unknown.

WHAT ARE THE UNINTENDED MESSAGES WE ARE SENDING?

When I hear people reacting defensively, I get the message that they are just denying some issue in their lives. Or, they are just scared of all the unknowns of changing. They wouldn't react so strongly if the issue didn't carry some element of truth. At least that is my suspicion, probably because that is true when I react so strongly against changing. I think other people are acting like I do.

I also get the message that they just don't care about me or my ideas. They are not even willing to engage in a dialogue about the issue. They just want to slough it off. If this is an issue that I care deeply about, it hurts me when they just jump into a Don't Change Me Game.

WHAT ARE SOME LOVING SOLUTIONS TO REPLACE THESE GAMES?

Be willing to change, to work on improving your life. Get over your fear of the unknowns of changing. Remember, not changing creates its own set of unknowns. Just do it!

How's that working for you?

Maybe not too well, especially if you still have this desire to control your life. Make your plan, work your plan, and fulfill your plan—isn't that the American way? You are in control of your destiny, and it is up to you to make your life the life you've always wanted. You only change the areas in your life that you want to change, the ones that are needed to fulfill your plan.

Let's flip this idea on its head. What if we recognize we are not in control? What if we don't resent that fact, but actually relish and celebrate our lack of control? What if we yield control to the personal creator of the universe and trust his control over our lives? What if we take each area of possible change and ask him if now is the time for us to be more loving in that area of our lives? Or, talk about it with your friends—where can I change to be more caring and authentic?

I have this two-pronged theory:

- It is more effective for me to judge my own shortcomings and to try to improve myself than it is to judge others and try to change them. This theory seems consistent with Jesus' warning to be careful about judging others—first remove the log in your own eye before trying to remove the speck from someone else's eye (Matt 7:3).

- At the same time, to live in relationship with another person means encouraging one another to grow, which includes giving advice on how to improve our lives together. We can't control the other person's life or decisions. We can try to become more loving people. Throughout their lives, Jesus and Paul (one of the New Testament writers) gave others advice on living more God-pleasing and loving lives. So when I talk with others about how I can become more loving, that is actually a helpful (even if an unsettling) exercise.

If God leads us to work on one area of our lives, we don't have to slough off suggestions from others with superficial Don't Change Me Games. Instead of playing a Don't Change Me Game with the person who is "pressuring" us to change, we can actually dialogue about where God is working in our lives. We don't have to take it as unfair criticism—we can actually ponder the other person's ideas and respond with our real feelings and thoughts. We can exchange ideas without taking it so personally. We can trust God that they will accept us anyway. At least we know God accepts us anyway.

In the dialogue with the one "pressuring" us to change, God may open our eyes to another area to change, one we had not even noticed before, one that is actually critical to change now. If not, we can share that point directly with the advisor. As long as we are open to God speaking into our lives, either answer may be okay. God works through the eyes and ears and ideas of our friends. We don't have to be in control. We can let go of the outcome. What a relief!

Maybe we could even apply some of the Twelve Steps of Alcoholics Anonymous to change, substituting "changing" for "alcohol":

- We admitted we were powerless over [changing our lives]—that our lives had become unmanageable.
- [We] came to believe that a Power greater than ourselves could restore us to sanity.
- [We] made a decision to turn our will and our lives over to the care of God *as we understood him.*
- [We] made a searching and fearless moral inventory of ourselves.
- [We] admitted to God, to ourselves, and to another human being the exact nature of our wrongs.
- [We] were entirely ready to have God remove all these defects of character.

- [We] humbly asked him to remove our shortcomings.
- [We] made a list of all persons we had harmed, and became willing to make amends to them all.
- [We] made direct amends to such people wherever possible, except when to do so would injure them or others.
- [We] continued to take personal inventory and when we were wrong promptly admitted it.
- [We] sought through prayer and meditation to improve our conscious contact with God, *as we understood him*, praying only for knowledge of his will for us and the power to carry that out.
- Having had a spiritual awakening as the result of these Steps, we tried to carry this message to [others who are addicted to not changing], and to practice these principles in all our affairs.[1]

While these twelve steps were designed to help alcoholics and drug addicts overcome their substance abuse, they are great guidelines to help all of us change and address our addictions to ourselves and to these relationship games we play. We can yield control and be willing to change aspects of our lives that God leads us to change.

WHAT ARE SOME POSITIVE ASPECTS OF THESE GAMES?

Certainly it doesn't help to just shut people off with "That's just the way I am" or "At least I am better than so-and-so" or "You don't understand me or this situation I am in." It doesn't help to accuse my friends of being judgmental without listening to their hearts.

On the other hand, I am a pleaser by nature. I know what it is like to spend my energy trying to keep everyone happy. Yielding control of my life and my decisions to someone else, in the name of letting them make me a more loving person (in their mold), is just shifting control to another person, not to God. So it is healthy to not automatically follow every person's suggestion for my life—just don't use Don't Change Me Games to stop the dialogue.

I do have to discern where God is leading me to change, not where you are leading me to change. If you and several other friends are giv-

---

1. A. A. World Services, Inc., "Twelve Steps."

ing me the same message, I should wake up and listen—God could be speaking through you. Oh God, give me wisdom and a listening heart!

SO HOW ABOUT YOU?

1. What stories do you have like these? In other words, what Don't Change Me Games do you see other people playing (either ones listed in this chapter or others you can think of)? What Don't Change Me Games do you play?

2. I believe Don't Change Me Gamers don't seek advice very often. So how about you—how often do you actually seek another person's advice?

    a. I hardly ever ask someone else for advice

    b. Once per week

    c. Once per day

    d. More than once per day

3. I also don't believe Don't Change Me Gamers follow other people's advice very often, even if they ask for advice. So how about you—how often do you actually follow another person's advice (either advice you asked for or unsolicited advice)?

    a. I hardly ever follow someone else's advice

    b. Once per week

    c. Once per day

    d. More than once per day

4. What would life look like if you didn't play Don't Change Me Games?

3

Avoiding Responsibility Games

I don't want to experience the painful consequences of my actions, so I protect myself by blaming others for my circumstances (with an Avoiding Responsibility Game). Instead of playing this game, I will accept the outcome of my role in this situation, state my fears, and apologize if appropriate.

Beth and I co-lead (with three other couples) a support group for parents whose children are making destructive decisions (drugs, alcohol, cutting, anorexia, etc.). We have found some similarities among our children who are dealing with their addictions. One similarity is their tendency to avoid the consequences of their decisions by not telling the truth, at least not all of the truth. Honest people call this "lying." You may have heard the joke: "How do you know when an addict is lying? You know he is lying when his lips are moving."

Here's my observation about avoiding responsibility: You don't have to suffer from these obvious addictions to alcohol, drugs, etc. to play an Avoiding Responsibility Game. "Regular people," like you and me, play these games, too. (Maybe we "regular people" just have less obvious, more socially acceptable addictions.)

For example, if you are like me, you have your excuse (= lie) ready if you ever get caught speeding while driving on the highway. You know you are breaking the law, but you don't want to pay the penalty if you are caught. You want to avoid the responsibility by lying to the police officer about your knowledge of the speed limit or your broken speedometer. Your "avoiding responsibility" list of planned lies goes on. Which one will fit this situation? If the police officer gives you a speeding ticket anyway, then you hire a lawyer to try to convince the judge to "let you off this time." You even complain about the time it takes to go to court, "It's so unfair." As if you shouldn't be held responsible for breaking the law.

If you want to try to avoid responsibility for your actions, lying is always an option. Let's look at some more subtle approaches, or games you might play instead of lying. Avoiding Responsibility Games give you permission to avoid responsibility for your actions (what a creative name for these games!), which you already recognize are illegal or unloving. A couple of examples of these games are:

- Blame Game
- Pump Fake Apology Games

In a sense, the Avoiding Responsibility Games are similar to the Don't Change Me Games. The Avoiding Responsibility Games primarily protect you from having to be accountable for past decisions and actions, while the Don't Change Me Games protect you from being accountable for future actions (or inaction).

> **THE LIFEBOAT ANALOGY**
>
> Donald Miller writes about two related analogies that have helped me see when I am playing a game:
>
> - I am made to be told by God who I am. You are made this way, too. When Adam and Eve were in the Garden of Eden, their identities were determined by what God told them about themselves. When their relationship with God was broken, they began looking to each other to tell them who they were. Like Adam and Eve, without listening to God, I keep looking to other people to define my identity.
> - I feel this intensely in my relationships and day-to-day activities. It is like I am living in the middle of that values-clarification exercise we learned in high school—the one where six people are in a lifeboat. In the exercise, the lifeboat might contain a disabled person, an older woman, a young child, a preacher, a lawyer, and a teacher. Each student has to determine which passenger gets thrown overboard, so the rest can live.

> - In my life I act as if I am one of the passengers on the lifeboat, and the other passengers on the lifeboat have to determine who will be thrown overboard. I keep trying to justify my existence to the fellow passengers in my circle of relationships, so they will not vote me off the lifeboat. I am not just looking to others to define my identity, but it really is a matter of life and death—I have to prove my value to you to live.[1]

That is so me! I relish the times when others compliment my work or my choices, and I dread the times when they feel like I have let them down. After reading this analogy, I started seeing clearly that what other people thought of me also defined me. I started seeing it in others, too, as they tried to justify themselves to the people around them. Not only did I see it, but I also felt it—felt it deeply. And when I feel the need to protect myself, I am most tempted to play one of these games. This analogy is so helpful in clarifying my intentions that you will find references to the lifeboat throughout this book.

I actually had a little epiphany regarding the lifeboat analogy. In general, I considered confident, even arrogant people as not being afraid of anything. I thought that type person didn't try to protect himself from some underlying fear. So why would he play games to protect himself? Miller's lifeboat analogy brought the truth home to me—he is trying to protect himself, too. His confidence and arrogance are his ways to protect his self-worth, securing his seat on the lifeboat.

Even writing this book brought up some lifeboat feelings for me. While I have this pure motive for writing the book (to help myself and others live more honestly and with more love), I also have thought about what others would say after reading the book. I could picture them saying, "Oh Joe. I didn't know you could write, too." Or maybe, "I really liked the style—the way you mixed humor into the messages. And whoever would have thought to name these games. Did you do that?" Maybe even, "I found your book so helpful in identifying the games I play. You have helped me so much."

---

1. Miller, *Searching*, 91–95, 105–118.

> Of course, I would politely blush and say, "You know, these ideas just come to me. I can't really control my brain or these ideas. I believe they must come from God." All the while I would be feeling securely in the lifeboat. These imaginary people are defining my identity with their comments, and their praises are telling me I am respected and accepted. If imaginary people can do that, just think how the comments and thoughts of real people can create my identity.

PLAYING THE BLAME GAME

In the Blame Game, I am the victim of my circumstances. Any challenges or problems in my life are caused by someone else mistreating me. For some people, God is ultimately the problem—why did he make me this way? For example:

- I get a speeding ticket, and it's all because the county government needs to hit its revenue target for the month. Besides, a car just passed me five minutes ago doing eighty miles per hour—the cop should have pulled him, not me.

- A female peer at work gets promoted instead of me. Obviously, the company needed to meet its quota of women managers, and unfortunately, I am not a woman.

- Our child is doing drugs because of the other kids she hangs out with. They are a bad influence on her. If she had better friends, she would be behaving better. Meanwhile, our child is also probably playing another Blame Game—smoking pot is legal in many other countries. Our laws are backward and unfair—smoking pot is then okay in our child's mind.

Often, the main issue for gamers who play the Blame Game is to avoid getting caught. Somehow I have justified in my mind that my actions are okay. While my actions may be illegal, against company policy, or unloving, everyone else does it or that person deserved it. When I am challenged or caught, it's not my fault. I am the victim.

A related, more subtle way to play the Blame Game is to agree that I am partially at fault, but obviously not the major cause of the problem. I have some kind of problem or challenge in my life or my family's life.

I see that part of the problem could be my fault, or at least some other people could think it is my fault. They might vote me off the lifeboat. I certainly don't want to be blamed for the entire problem—it is certainly not all my fault. If I can work it out so only 30 to 40 percent of the blame is mine and the majority of the blame belongs to someone else, I will win the Blame Game. I won't be the one voted off the lifeboat—the other person will.

Beth and I play this game sometimes, especially when we have miscommunicated about some issue. For example:

Beth: Why are you just now getting home? I told you this morning that we have a dinner with the Smiths tonight at 6:30 in Greensboro.

Joe: I heard you say we had a dinner with them at 6:30, but I didn't hear you say we were going to Greensboro.

Beth: I am sure I said we were going to that new restaurant in Greensboro when we were talking. Weren't you reading the paper when we were talking? I bet you weren't listening.

Joe: You know, when you were telling me about our dinner from the other room, the garbage truck was outside making a lot of noise, so maybe that is why I didn't hear you. Or you might have just been mumbling—you know, you are doing that more and more lately.

Beth: Well, I think you need to get your ears checked. You hear less and less every day.

Wow! Look at the blame shifting back and forth. We don't really know why I didn't get the message, but we sure are devoting a lot of energy into figuring out why—we need to sort out the blame. Each of us wants to have less than 50 percent of the blame, to prove that someone else is primarily at fault.

I can also elevate the Blame Game to another level by going on the offensive, especially if it looks like I am losing the argument. I typically bring in other "facts" to support my case that I am not totally at fault. The conversation goes from a seemingly rational assignment of blame to a "get off my back" offensive counterattack. I even bring up "facts" from previous disagreements to justify my point that this is not totally my fault. Emotions start flying.

In our example above, you can see that Beth and I were shifting from blaming each other for this specific problem to adding other "going on the offensive" counterattacks. Beth accused me of not listening,

I accused her of mumbling, and she reminded me that my hearing was getting worse. Subtly, we are attacking each other, while appearing to sort out the root cause of our current problem.

Going on the offensive is often not this subtle. Our conversation could have gone like this:

> Beth: [*repeating her lines, so we can remember how this conversation started*] Why are you just now getting home? I told you this morning that we have a dinner with the Smiths tonight at 6:30 in Greensboro.
>
> Joe: Well, I am ready to go right now. I can wear my clothes from work. But you don't look like you're ready. You have on jeans and your hair doesn't look right. Even if I had been home earlier, you still wouldn't be ready. This is the way it always works [*a "fact" from a previous argument, justifying my point*]. You get on me when you are the one holding us up. How much longer are you going to be anyway?

I have shifted the attention now to Beth by going on the offensive. If this works, the pressure is off me. Beth is on the defensive, and at least for the moment I am still hanging on in the lifeboat.

THE PLACE FOR THE NOT-SO-WHITE LIE

A white lie is defined as "an often trivial, diplomatic or well-intentioned untruth."[2] A typical white lie might be, "No, you don't look fat in that outfit."

I find that when I play the Avoiding Responsibility Games, I am tempted to justify my argument with a not-so-white lie if I think it would be helpful and it would be hard to prove it is a lie. I already have my planned list of excuses for speeding (= lies), which the police officer can't really disprove. I am not sure I could classify these not-so-white lies as "trivial, diplomatic, or well-intentioned," except that I consider them trivial, and they are well-intended to keep me out of trouble. That's why they are called "not-so-white" lies.

---

2. *American Heritage Dictionary*, s.v. "white lie," accessed May 17, 2011, http://www.answers.com/topic/white-lie.

> In the above example, the trash truck may have come by sometime while I was eating breakfast, but I have no idea whether it was making extra noise when we were discussing our plans for the evening. It just helps support my argument, and the truck could have come by during our conversation. No harm, no foul, as they say in basketball. Funny thing—how I can justify that type of lying as trivial and yet get so upset when other people lie to me?
>
> And who knows? Beth could be lying, too, when she says she is so sure she mentioned we were going to Greensboro. I can't refute her memory. Another funny thing—if I am used to telling not-so-white lies in this situation, I automatically assume Beth could be lying, too. If I would do it, I assume (with my ESP) that she would, too.
>
> You know, maybe these are not really "funny things." The irony is not that funny. Maybe the more appropriate word is "sad."

PLAYING THE PUMP FAKE APOLOGY GAME

I love to play basketball. My success in basketball is limited by my genes. While a good basketball player may be tall but slow or short but quick, I am short but slow. So if I have an open shot, a taller player on the other team can pretty easily block my shot. In that situation I will try to first make a "pump fake." I act like I am going to shoot the ball, when I really don't plan to shoot the ball yet. Hopefully, the tall defender on the other team is faked out, jumps up to block my shot, and I dribble around him for an open shot.

In the Pump Fake Apology Games, I act like I am apologizing. I hope the other person is faked out and thinks I have apologized, so she is no longer upset at me. This is a popular game for me to play after playing the Blame Game. I inevitably realize that my relationship with another person is now strained. I still believe I am right, or at least mostly right, but I want to heal the relationship. At least I want to relieve the tension and move on with the rest of my life. So I act like I am apologizing, but I can't bring myself to admit much fault. Actually, it can just be another way to play the Blame Game—acting like I am assuming some blame when I really am not assuming much responsibility at all.

The best example of a Pump Fake Apology was Julia Duffy's character on the 1980s television series *Newhart*. She played the role of Stephanie Vanderkellen, a spoiled maid working at Newhart's bed and breakfast. Whenever she was caught doing something incorrectly or lazily, she recognized the need to apologize. In her typical apology, she tossed her blonde hair to one side, avoided making eye contact, and quickly and flippantly said, "Sorry, sorry, sorry." Once her quick apology was finished, she assumed she could move on to the next item on her agenda, and she proceeded to do so without waiting for any response from the other person.

So have you done that—tried to give a quick "Sorry" (maybe while looking down at the floor), hoping that this pump fake apology would be enough? How did that work out for you? Based on my experience, this flippant "Sorry" approach is not effective. So I have more sophisticated approaches. For example:

- "I'm sorry you feel hurt." Notice that I am not sorry for anything I said or did. Instead, I am sorry that you have these negative feelings, without taking any responsibility for my part in this situation.

- "I'm sorry if I offended you." The key word here is "if." This approach is close to "Sorry, sorry, sorry." I am not willing to take the time to find out your real feelings—did I offend you, hurt you, frustrate you, or what? What could I have done differently? I don't care enough to find out. I am sorry that we have this tension between us, and I really hope this Pump Fake Apology is enough to resolve the issue, because I don't want to deal with it anymore.

- "I didn't mean to hurt you." Since it wasn't my intention to hurt you, I am not even sure I need to apologize. I could have accidentally dropped a heavy weight on your toe, or I could have just said something "innocently" that hurt your feelings. Either way, I don't apologize unless I actually meant to hurt you.

- "I'm sorry that I said that about you, but I just had a bad day at work." I call this the But Pump Fake Apology. The "but" just renders the first part of the sentence (the apology part) meaningless. All the other person hears is the second part of the sentence after the "but," which is my rationalization for my actions. We are back in the Blame Game, just using the But Apology to point out that I don't have that much fault for this problem.

Even these more sophisticated approaches are not always effective in helping me avoid responsibility. One thing for certain—they certainly aren't effective in healing my relationships.

WHERE DO WE FEEL THREATENED? HOW DO WE TRY TO PROTECT OURSELVES WITH THESE GAMES?

What is the deal with accepting responsibility? Do we just not want to accept the consequences of our decisions? I think that is part of the problem, but I don't think that is our biggest threat.

Do we just not want to admit we are human—that we make mistakes? I don't think we are threatened by our humanity—in general terms, we all admit we are not perfect. But maybe that is a logical confession that has no specific consequences or feelings of failure. We just have a hard time admitting that we aren't perfect in each situation, because the specific situation includes the obvious, immediate consequences and all the negative emotions—our fears, our frustrations, our failure.

Beth thinks that admitting she is at fault in a specific situation shows she could not even live up to her own expectations for herself—she has let herself down—and that is the ultimate blow to her self-esteem (or pride). This gets personal and emotional for her, so she tends to jump into the Blame Game.

When I play an Avoiding Responsibility Game, to some extent I am protecting myself against being misunderstood. I am worried about how people will interpret (more likely misinterpret) this problem. I really am better than I appear in this situation. I am not normally the type of person who breaks the law, so this speeding ticket is an exception. I really am a good worker at my job—not getting the promotion does not reflect on how dumb I am or how lazy I am at work. I really am a good parent, and my child is really a decent kid—don't let her drug issues reflect badly on her or on me.

I also wonder if playing an Avoiding Responsibility Game is a reflection of how we treat people in similar situations. We assume others are going to blame us or criticize us when we fail, because that is what we would do to them. Therefore, we feel the need to defend ourselves against what we assume the other person is thinking. So we try to head it off with an Avoiding Responsibility Game.

WHAT ARE THE UNINTENDED MESSAGES WE ARE SENDING?

Ironically, I think we often send the very message that we are trying to avoid sending. In the Blame Game, I may not want the other person to speculate that I am really not that good a person. I don't want to be misunderstood—I am really smarter, more caring, etc., than this problem makes me look. So when I play this game, trying to point out others' share of the blame, what do you think comes to the mind of the other person? Maybe "Wow! He sure is being defensive. I wonder what he is trying to hide."

Or in the example of my being late to go to dinner, I don't want Beth to think I don't care about her. So I get in an argument playing the Blame Game, which then escalates the issue even further. Ironically, after this verbal exchange, she really won't think I care about her.

WHAT ARE SOME LOVING SOLUTIONS TO REPLACE THESE GAMES?

As I mentioned earlier, I have found it freeing to start stating my fears, rather than trying to work around them. This works if I am aware enough of my fears before I start reacting to the situation. Or at least if I am aware of my fears during my reaction and I can reorient myself.

For this process to work, I have to also reorient my thinking to see that being transparent is good for me and my relationships. That takes faith—faith that other people won't take advantage of my openness. Or faith that God will work it out for his good, even if others do take advantage of me.

It is also helpful to identify my emotions. This process helps me identify what I am going through at this point, and makes it less likely that I will resort to one of these games.

In a couple of the above examples, my responses could be the following:

- You know, I am feeling so stupid for speeding, especially in this town known for its speed traps. My mind was wandering and I didn't even notice the speed limit changed. I am really worried about admitting to my wife that I got caught speeding—$150 down the drain. Plus our insurance will go up. I am so ticked at myself!

- My daughter is hooked on drugs, and I don't know what to do. When I saw other kids struggling, I wondered where their parents went wrong. Now I wonder about myself and what others think about our family. Or maybe it's her friends who are to blame. Of course, she chooses her friends. I feel so hopeless and helpless.

In each of these examples, I have spoken my fears and my feelings (either out loud or in self-talk). I admit that I am not good sorting all this out at the time. More often I have to work through the situation later—taking advantage of 20–20 hindsight after things have calmed down.

I believe the Blame Game was the first game I identified in our marriage. I found myself defending Beth's counterattacks on several points, all in the same disagreement. I couldn't win. It never occurred to me that her identity (or even my identity) was at stake. I just knew that saying that she was going on the offensive with a Blame Game took some of the power out of her arguments.

Once you really want to apologize (going beyond the Pump Fake Apology), I suggest that you have to let go of the other person's share of the blame or your idea of the other factors involved. Make your apology for your part of the problem and just stop talking. Let the other person respond. Reflectively listen. Don't defend yourself—just try to understand the other person's view.

WHAT ARE SOME POSITIVE ASPECTS OF THESE GAMES?

Sorting out root causes of our problems is a helpful exercise, especially if it helps us avoid the same problem in the future. Actually, you are using some aspect of the Blame Game when you read this book, figure out what games you are playing, and use that information to avoid playing those games in the future. You are determining where you are at fault, and planning to act out of love the next time. Notice the difference. In this loving use of these aspects of the Blame Game, the focus is on how you can improve and avoid this problem in the future, not on assigning the majority of the blame to someone else. "What can *I* do to avoid this problem next time?" seems to be a good topic for reflection or discussion.

"What can *we* do to avoid this problem next time?" can also be helpful. Just recognize that the intention in our hearts is what matters. If we are trying to justify staying in the lifeboat, we can even manipulate this "we" discussion to become a defensive Blame Game.

HUMAN ERROR

For Beth and me, one root cause of our disagreements is "human error." We can start blaming each other for mistakes we each made, which are just the result of being human. I drop the yogurt on the floor, Beth forgets to use the $10-off coupon at the grocery store, we both accidentally leave the heater set too high while on vacation, etc. No inappropriate motives. Neither one intended to act in a hurtful way. Maybe each of us was just careless or forgetful or not thinking through what we were doing, but it's just human error. Recognizing this fact, we have become more patient with each other's mistakes.

Unfortunately, sometimes we play an ESP Game and read some selfish intentions into these human mistakes. Beth can speculate that I made this careless mistake because I am too self-focused or too focused on work. Thus, I am not just careless but actually I am inconsiderate and don't care about her. Remembering the advice in chapter 2 on the ESP Games, Beth could apply the principle, "Give him the benefit of the doubt and then check it out." Then after talking to me, she has to decide whether to believe how I have responded/defended myself. Of course, it is up to me to actually tell the truth when she questions if I was overly self-focused—was I really shutting her and everyone else out when we had expected to spend some time together that day?

At least we know our tendencies, by identifying some root causes for our arguments. And we see how we can overreact to human errors and start speculating about the other person's motives. With that knowledge, we have a better chance of avoiding these arguments in the future.

SO HOW ABOUT YOU?

1. What stories do you have like these? In other words, what Avoiding Responsibility Games do you see other people playing (either ones listed in this chapter or others you can think of)? What Avoiding Responsibility Games do you play?

2. It seems obvious—people who play Avoiding Responsibility Games rarely admit to others that they are wrong. How often do you admit to others you are wrong in your opinions or statements or actions?

    a. I rarely ever admit I am wrong
    b. Once per week
    c. Once per day
    d. More than once per day

3. How often do you feel you are being misunderstood and need to defend yourself from what others may be thinking?

    a. Rarely
    b. Once per week
    c. Once per day
    d. More than once per day

4. What would life look like if you didn't play Avoiding Responsibility Games?

4

Isolation Games

I am concerned about getting hurt or embarrassed, so I protect myself by not disclosing my real thoughts and emotions (with an Isolation Game). Instead of playing this game, I will connect with you by sharing my feelings, my stories, my hopes, and my disappointments.

I WAS FLYING ON an airplane to meet two of my sons (Brent and David) for a week together on vacation. I decided to read John Eldredge's *Wild at Heart* on the long flight. His points about the typical weaknesses in our fathering really touched my heart.[1] I remember taking notes. I remember crying, too, thinking about my own father and about my three sons.

In the book, Eldredge suggests asking your children what they are (were) afraid to talk to you about.[2] Being an achiever, I wanted to be as good a father as I could be, even if my sons were living on their own. So at a quiet moment one evening, I took the risk and asked each of them that question. Brent responded with the penetrating words I will never forget, "You know, Dad, I never wanted to tell you when I messed up—like when I made mistakes at school or in my personal life. I think I never wanted to talk about my mistakes, because I never thought you made any mistakes."

I still relive that wrenching feeling each time I tell this story. It was like a knife had been stuck in my back. I felt so awful. Of course, I had made mistakes. By playing Isolation Games, I never shared those mistakes with my sons. I might share some with Beth, but what good would

---

1. Eldredge, *Wild at Heart*, 69–75.
2. Ibid., 112.

it do to share them with my sons? How could my sons help me solve these problems? So short-sighted, so stupid . . . so isolated.

You can tell from this story—I am the master at games of isolation. It comes naturally to introverts like me, who theoretically need "alone time" to regenerate our energy. Ironically, even writing this book about relationships seems like a way to escape relating to others, including Beth. At times, I wonder if I will ever feel like coming out of my shell to share what I am thinking or feeling—it always feels so risky.

Larry Crabb can relate to my desire to isolate myself, to avoid the risk of opening myself up to others. He points out: "Selfishness, at its root, is self-protectiveness. Our primary commitment is to make certain no one can hurt us. The best way to do that is to never be fully vulnerable. That's the first commandment of fallen [Isolation Game] thinking: *Trust no one and you shall live.*"[3]

If you are an extrovert, don't just skip this chapter. First, you probably want to recognize these games that your introverted friends play. Second, you still might see yourself in the I Don't Care Game.

I have included two sample Isolation Games:

- Turtle Shell Game
- I Don't Care Game

PLAYING THE TURTLE SHELL GAME

This is a simple game to play—just withdraw into your shell. Don't share anything meaningful about what you are thinking or feeling. Don't trust others. Talk about the news, sports, work projects, ideas, history, and even other people—just don't disclose yourself. Keep to the facts.

Or, if you are in ministry, just listen to others. Let them disclose. Just don't share your own stuff. Nobody needs to know your struggles—it wouldn't help them anyway. (Or would it?)

Or you may remember your mom telling you "to be an interesting person, you need to be interested in other people." You may have translated her advice to only ask questions, so the other person will talk about himself. Then he will like you, and maybe not so coincidentally, you will have revealed so little about yourself that he cannot find fault with you.

You can even become self-righteous while playing the Turtle Shell Game. You look down on those extroverts who share every detail about

---

3. Crabb, *Shattered Dreams*, 18.

their lives. You say to yourself, "He is so pompous, to think that all of us want to hear all this mundane stuff about himself. I would never be so bold to bore others like that." Thus, you rationalize that the Turtle Shell Game is actually a morally better way to live.

Hey . . . I am right there with you. I prefer to stay on the sidelines in conversations. Just observe, while others talk. At the opportune moment, after thinking about what I am going to say, I throw out some idea that is helpful—if not helpful, then thought-provoking or witty (more about adding humor to this game later). Since I mulled over what I was going to say, I can feel rather confident I won't look stupid when I say it. I may even look wise. I feel no need to share much about myself. I can't see that my issues help them solve their problems, and I am not sure they can help me solve my stuff—too painful to bring up anyway.

Those who have perfected this game can avoid responding to the most probing questions about even the toughest issues. For example, George and Jay are close friends who go fishing together a couple of times each month. Here is a recent conversation:

George: I heard from your wife that you were having a heart stress test.

Jay: Yep.

George: Well, what did they find?

Jay: I have one artery blocked. [*pauses, then opens up a little*] I have to have some heart procedure at the doctor's office on Friday. They didn't want to wait until next week.

George: How do you feel about having that procedure so quickly?

Jay: Well, I guess it's what needs to happen. Gotta get the old ticker fixed somehow.

George: You don't sound worried.

Jay: Not much worry can do about it.

George: Thanks for sharing.

It's a funny thing—I bet Jay really struggled sharing that the doctor didn't want to wait until next week to perform the heart operation. While he felt he was sharing intimately (that one detail about his surgery), he had a chance to disclose much more to his friend. Notice that he answered George's questions with short sentences. He never really said if he is worried or how he got to this point of not worrying. For some of us, this conversation shows how natural it is to share as little as possible about ourselves.

Here is a way to add humor to the Turtle Shell Game. I never reveal my feelings or much of my inner self. Instead, I just tell humorous stories or make some witty comment as part of the conversation. The witty comment doesn't reveal anything about me. If I tell a funny story, it may be about someone else, or it may be about me. If it's about me, my humorous story will typically be about some past event, where I made a stupid or silly (= humorous) decision. That has an additional benefit, because it makes me look humble and transparent, when the event actually occurred so long ago that I am over it and I am not really dealing with any pain or emotions by sharing it now.

I can take the Turtle Shell Game to another level by just shutting down. As you recall, I don't win too many verbal arguments with Beth, since she thinks more quickly and verbalizes her thoughts better than I do. After she makes her point, I mull it over without saying anything. I think through what I am going to say before I say it. I actually think about how she might react to what I plan to say, and then I modify my words so they best reflect what I am thinking. I don't want to say something stupid that escalates this issue even further.

Since I don't like to disclose myself, I even try to hide the fact that I am playing a Turtle Shell Game. I can be purposely vague in my discussions with Beth, giving her a "cloudy response." I respond in a way that Beth cannot really know what I am saying. I either avoid her question by:

- answering a different question, or
- asking a question as my response, or
- using vague sarcasm to cloud my answer.

Cloudy Response No. 1—Answering a Different Question

We have all seen politicians avoid revealing their opinions by answering a debate question with an answer that really doesn't answer the question. That is their version of a cloudy response. Here is an example from my experience:

> Beth: I was thinking about us getting together for dinner with the Browns at Joe's Chicken House on Friday. We haven't seen them in a while. What do you think about this idea for Friday night?
>
> Joe: Well, you know I always enjoy eating at Joe's Chicken House.

Notice that I didn't really answer the total question. I didn't say if I wanted to get with the Browns or not. I didn't even say if I had some other ideas about Friday night. Mission: Isolation accomplished!

Cloudy Response No. 2—Answering a Question with a Question

Answering a question with a question is typically a safe way to give a cloudy response. One of my favorite examples is recorded in the 1984 television movie *A Christmas Carol*—the one where George C. Scott plays Ebenezer Scrooge. Scrooge and Belle are engaged to be married, but they have been waiting until Scrooge earns enough money to support the two of them. It is a snowy day in London, and Belle has been waiting patiently to meet Scrooge at a park bench. He shows up late, running to try to make up for it, apparently delayed by a business deal. Scrooge is well-dressed, which shows he has been successful during this time, perhaps successful enough that they could have already been married. We get the impression that he is now more devoted to success in business than to anything else or anyone else, including Belle. During the conversation, Belle asks the question that has been bothering her:

> Belle: Knowing what you know now, Ebenezer, with the position you now enjoy, would you still pursue me, a poor, dowry-less woman?
>
> Ebenezer: [*giving a cloudy response by answering her specific request with his own non-committal question*] You think I would not pursue you now?
>
> Belle: Oh, Ebenezer. What a safe but terrible answer!

In the movie, Belle walks off, leaving Ebenezer standing alone, while he deals with his conflicting emotions and the shock of being caught playing this Isolation Game.[4] Since watching this movie, Beth has used this line to call me out for playing this game, saying "Oh, Joe. What a safe but terrible answer!"

Cloudy Response No. 3—Being Vague with Sarcasm

I can also use humor to cloud my emotions or feelings, even while participating in the conversation. I leave my response open to interpretation and may only reveal my real thoughts once I gauge your reaction to my unrevealing, often sarcastic answer. Using the previous Joe's Chicken House example:

---

4. *A Christmas Carol.*

Beth: I was thinking about us getting together for dinner with the Browns at Joe's Chicken House on Friday. We haven't seen them in a while. What do you think about this idea for Friday night?

Joe: Oh yeah. We had such an interesting time with the Browns the last time we got together. [*said in a deadpan manner, so Beth can't really tell whether I mean that it really was interesting (as in a positive way) or interesting (as in a nice way to say some negative comment, like it really was weird or boring)*]

Beth: Well, she told me they have been struggling lately with their son's addiction to drugs. Are you saying you don't find them interesting? Or what exactly are you saying? [*challenging my cloudy response*]

Joe: [*realizing that Beth really does want to get with the Browns and seeing that our time together might be useful to them, I jump into the pleasing mode*] I think that does sound interesting. Maybe we can help them. That works for me. [*still ignoring her question and never really admitting whether I was being sarcastic or truthful in my first comment about the last get-together being "interesting"*]

Now, it's back in Beth's court. Is it really worth her energy to draw out of me what I really meant by "interesting"? Obviously, I hope I have pleased her enough by agreeing with the Friday night plans that it is not worth further discussion on the topic. If so, I have used a sarcastic cloudy response to isolate myself, without really even figuring out what I meant or disclosing that to Beth.

> **OUR WRITTEN ARGUMENT**
> **(DESIGNED WITH THE INTROVERT IN MIND)**
>
> Beth and I had a written argument once and it worked out well for us. We had started an argument at the Charlotte airport, where we were meeting someone else for a flight to attend a wedding in El Salvador.
>
> Our arguments are often tied to some trip out of town. We have speculated that we are both rushing around, and something goes haywire in the preparations. We haven't spent much time together, so we turn the issue into an argument. Or, I am still trying to take care of some last-minute work issues on the trip, while Beth has already finished her chores. Since she has finished, she thinks I also should be finished taking care of these urgent (often work-related) issues.

> In any case, we were not happy with each other when we boarded the airplane. Beth was feeling ignored and thinking that I was treating this other person rudely, and I was feeling unfairly criticized. This was a situation ripe for an argument. The problem was we didn't feel comfortable resolving our tension out loud, in front of all these other airline passengers.
>
> Since I don't remember whose idea it was, it must have been Beth's idea—we started writing on a notebook what we were thinking and feeling. We each took turns and had to wait until the other person was finished to read and react. It worked well for someone like me, who likes to think before responding (the Turtle Shell Game). I felt much more comfortable thinking through my thoughts and feelings before writing them down. I didn't feel rushed. Beth seemed to get into the written-argument process, too. By the time we landed in El Salvador, we had resolved our issues enough to enjoy each other and a delightful wedding.
>
> I really should suggest writing out our arguments again, even when the situation doesn't force us to do so. It certainly helps an introvert like me.

PLAYING THE I DON'T CARE GAME

The I Don't Care Game is another example of an Isolation Game. Instead of admitting that I am angry or hurt by someone, I respond by saying to myself, "I don't care." I isolate myself from the pain of the situation by acting like it is not a big deal. For example:

Larry: Matt, I know you worked hard over the last two weeks to set up our sports teams for tomorrow. It's late to let you know this, but I really can't play tomorrow. I have this commitment back home that I need to attend.

Matt: You're kidding me, right? It is six o'clock and you're just now letting me know! How long have you known about this conflict? Now that I think about it, it doesn't matter when you found out. I don't care anymore.

Larry: Let me see if I can find a replacement right now. [*He walks off*]

Matt: I give up. Here John, you figure these teams out. I don't care anymore. You guys work it out. [*Pauses*] I can't believe this is happening! But I don't care. I just don't care.

I remember playing this game as a teenager. This is how I used to respond when a girlfriend broke up with me—I would tell myself I didn't care. Somehow that seemed to work then—just go play some basketball with the guys and get over it that way. Pretend there is no pain.

We play a related I Don't Care Game almost every day as we watch the news on television. We are overwhelmed with stories about crimes, natural disasters, wars, etc. Some of these terrible events happen near us. Those are the ones that seem to impact me more. I can think of a tornado that plowed through a nearby neighborhood recently. What were my first thoughts? "Thank goodness that tornado didn't hit us. (In other words, this disaster didn't affect me, so my part of the world is still okay.) I hope the Red Cross takes care of these people. That would be so awful to have to hide out and wonder if we will survive this storm. Now I wonder what the next news item will cover—oh look, it's about this lady's art collection."

Look at how I isolated myself from the tornado victims' pain. I quickly moved on to the next news story, as long as this event did not personally affect me or my friends. In other words, this is not my problem. In this game, I really don't care. It's like I only have so much compassion to go around, and since I don't know the tornado victims personally, they don't qualify. I have become calloused to their pain. It doesn't even occur to me to think about how I could help them. They are not my problem—in this case, they are the Red Cross's problem.

I think it is the same feeling I get when I see a homeless person asking for money. To begin with, I don't trust him to really spend the money on food. Even further, my heart of compassion has been used up (it must be rather small). He is not my problem. I have isolated myself from the problems of anyone I don't know. The next step is to just isolate myself from the problems of the people I do know. It's a slippery slope leading me to only care about my own issues. No one besides me matters.

A friend suggested that the words that go through his mind are, "I'm glad that's not me." He related the story from his childhood where he saw a girl fall down some stairs at school. He distinctly remembers his first reaction, "Glad that wasn't me." While we were discussing this memory, he looked ahead at his wife walking in front of us. She was perspiring in an embarrassing place on her pants, and true to form, he pointed at her pants and said, "Glad that's not me." We laughed at the irony of the situation—still automatically playing this same, unloving game as adults. In that situation, it was easier to laugh at the irony than it was to cry in remorse.

Here is some real irony:

- When I'm hurt by someone and claim "I don't care" about some painful issue, many times I really do care, even though I say I don't. I'm trying to use this attitude to avoid the pain.
- When I watch the tragedies on the news, I really don't care, even though I talk like I do. At least I don't care enough to do anything besides talk to myself about how awful these unfortunate people must be feeling. Or I just say to myself, "Glad that's not me."

Don't get me wrong. I don't think I can solve the problems presented in every news story. I don't feel capable to meet the needs of each homeless person I meet. But you know, I could ask God how he wants me to respond to these people and their needs. Maybe I can make a difference in the lives of a few of the people I encounter and stop playing the self-focused I Don't Care Game.

WHERE DO WE FEEL THREATENED? HOW DO WE TRY TO PROTECT OURSELVES WITH THESE GAMES?

I can speak to these games from personal experience. I play all the Isolation Games for the same reason—I don't want to deal with the pain (or potential pain) of letting others into my life. Intimacy may be a loving goal, but I feel vulnerable when I disclose myself. Can I really trust you to deal kindly with my dreams and my fears? Whether this is true or not, I feel safer when I withdraw, selectively disclose myself, and finally not care at all.

Emotions never helped me solve a problem anyway—they just seem to get in the way. I can't trust myself with my emotions. Why would I trust you with my emotions?

I have noticed a difference between Beth and me. She is an extrovert and I am an introvert. She talks more than I do. I tend to think through what I say before I say it. Beth works through her thoughts by saying them. From my observations, Beth says things that cause her to be criticized more often than I do. I think this has to do with her just saying more words than me. So applying probability theory, the more words I say, the more often I will say something that causes me to be the butt of a joke or causes me to be criticized—ultimately, to be humiliated.

I thus conclude that the less I say, the less often I will be humiliated. I rationalize playing the Turtle Shell Game and say as little as possible—I will portray myself as a good listener. If I do want to say something, I think through what I am planning to say, to be sure it sounds appropriate, thus reducing even further the chance I will be humiliated.

WHAT ARE THE UNINTENDED MESSAGES WE ARE SENDING?

Playing these isolation games can send several unintended messages:

- Most people assume we share ourselves with our friends. If I don't share some details about my life (including some of my emotions), the other person will assume she is just an acquaintance, not a real friend. I remember a client celebrating his retirement—a client with whom I had done a lot of consulting projects. I remember telling him how sorry I was when his father committed suicide. I would have said he was a friend. So I was surprised when he said at his retirement that he regretted that we really had not gotten to know each other very well. Looking back at the time I spent with him, I had never really opened up about my life to him.

- We only share ourselves with people we trust. If I don't share myself with you, you could assume that I just don't trust you.

- When I think through what I will say before I say it, I am trying to be certain that I am responding in the most honest and loving manner, or at least that my response doesn't betray some inappropriate feelings or thoughts. I suspect Beth questions the honesty of anything I say—I take so long to say it that it must be filtered. If filtered, can it be true?

- Playing the I Don't Care Game is a joke on me. The more I assert I don't care, the more it shows that I do care after all. I don't trust you or me enough to share what I really am feeling. I suspect others can figure out I really do care, despite what I am saying.

WHAT ARE SOME LOVING SOLUTIONS TO REPLACE THESE GAMES?

Just like the ESP Games, playing these Isolation Games feels emotionally safer. When you seek alternatives to playing the ESP Game, you risk your time and energy trying to understand the other person. When you seek alternatives to the Isolation Games, you risk sharing something very dear—yourself and your emotions. You make yourself even more vulnerable. Applying probability theory, the more you say, the more likely you will be humiliated.

Isn't that the point? Our greatest personal rewards come at the point of greatest risk. If you beat a child in a game of chess, what have you accomplished? If you go through life without experiencing the unconditional love of those who know the real you, have you really lived? While it feels safe to hide in your shell, shut down, and not care, you have also isolated yourself from a world of freedom—freedom to be yourself, to be vulnerable, to love and to be loved.

Brennan Manning observed a friend's parents, who lived in isolation from one another: "If he [Brennan's friend] had to write an epitaph for his parents' tombstone, it would say, 'Here lay two people who never knew one another.' His father could never share his feelings, so his mother never got to know him. To open yourself to another person, to stop lying about your loneliness, to stop lying about your fears and hurts, to be open about your affection, and to tell others how much they mean to you—that is the triumph of [the authentic person]."[5]

You are even missing the opportunity to be humbled when you have to admit what you just disclosed was illogical (that sounds better than being humiliated, doesn't it?) Funny thing—we want to be humble, but we don't want to be humbled or humiliated. Do we really think we will be become humble without being humiliated?

If I were reading this book, my immediate, play-it-safe response would be:

Reader: Thanks for the pep talk, Coach. What else have you got? You're going to need more than that to get me to spill my guts!

Joe: Sounds like this whole idea of sharing yourself, your thoughts and feelings, is still scary [*a little reflective listening*]. Or it doesn't fit your personality. Or it doesn't fit your idea of what real men or real women do.

---

5. Manning, *Souvenirs*, 128.

Reader: I share with my spouse/friend. Isn't that enough?

Joe: Really?

Reader: Well, yeah. Some of the time. When I feel like it. When it really matters.

Joe: Still seems to me that you're unsure that the benefits of coming out of your shell are worth the risk. You know, the unknown gain is not worth the known pain.

Reader: Maybe so. So were you listening, Mr. Reflective Listener? What else have you got?

Joe: Okay. See what you think of these two ideas for being less isolated and more engaged with others.

First, let's review our goal here—we are trying to develop more loving and authentic relationships. Our lives are more rewarding when love is a way of life. And these games (including the Isolation Games) can get in the way.

Second, you don't have to spill your guts to everyone you meet or even to everyone you know. You don't have time to do that and most people really don't want the extended answer to "How ya doing?"

Idea No. 1 for Overcoming Isolation

Gary Chapman suggests a realistic alternative to shutting down. He suggests sitting down with your spouse each day, and sharing three things that happened that day and how you felt about those events.[6]

That isn't so overwhelming, is it? If you're like me, you only know two feelings—I either feel good or bad. That's why I have had to spend time identifying my emotions, figuring out what my real feelings are (beyond good or bad). I don't like digging into my feelings, either—it seems easier to stick with the facts and move on to the next topic. I don't even like the way my gut churns when I relive the "bad" stuff that happened each day. I don't like reliving the pain.

Funny thing, though, when I do actually dig it back up and share it with Beth (or another close friend) and share what I felt when that happened, the event loses its power over me. I can more easily stop reliving it in my mind. I can more easily release the whole issue to God. If you play Isolation Games like me, you might want to see if this exercise helps you deal with emotional issues from the day.

6. Chapman, *Building Relationships*, 2.4–2.5.

Idea No. 2 for Overcoming Isolation

Your current life does not represent all of you. You have a story about your past and you probably have dreams about the future. Authentic relationships develop when we share our stories. Larry Crabb describes the process of sharing your story: "We really don't know each other very well. So many of our stories are never told. . . . So many of our struggles are never heard. . . . [While] the energy of love should permeate every relational encounter . . . not every conversation can (or should) center on soul-penetrating exchanges. . . . But if the story of your soul is *never* told, if the secrets of your heart are *never* shared, if the struggles in your life are *never* heard, then you are living the tragedy of an unobserved life."[7]

So can you do it? Ask another person about what life was like growing up. Or when he moved away. Or when he lost his job. "How was that for you?" is a great question, which gives the other person complete freedom to share anything—maybe their feelings, maybe not. Then share some of your story. How did you feel in that situation? How did you change (or not change) after that event?

We have a better chance of empathizing and patiently caring for each other, once we understand each other's stories. "So that's what it was like for you—I never even knew. You know, I felt the same way one time when . . . "

You may wonder what loving solution I implemented after hearing Brent tell me that he was afraid to share with me when he failed, because I had never shared with him when I failed. From that point on, I resolved to try to share both good and bad things with my sons when we talked—both areas of success and areas of failure and how I felt about them. It's still hard for me. I would prefer to stick with the facts and the good times. I have to ask God for the power to share, to guide my conversations. When I think about it, I even ask my son if he has had a "feeling thing" lately that he would like to share.

It's a whole different world now when I am talking with one of my sons. It's foggy here—it's not clear where I'm going—but I kind of like it . . . sometimes. I believe avoiding these games of isolation is what a life of love and authenticity is all about, so at times I step boldly into that fog and share more of myself.

---

7. Crabb, *Soul Talk*, 159-161.

WHAT ARE SOME POSITIVE ASPECTS OF THESE GAMES?

I have already pointed out that not everyone wants to know your stuff. Deciding to not share all your struggles and feelings in every encounter is okay, actually healthy. If you are an introvert like me, your tendency is to isolate yourself, naturally. It may not be a loving option, but it is such a safe option that you will rarely ask yourself, "When should I share less of myself?"

In my opinion, if you don't share when you've been hurt, don't try to reconcile a relationship, don't trust anyone with your story and your feelings, then you are playing an Isolation Game—to your detriment. So how do you know when to take the risk to share and when not to? Ask God. Trust your heart. Take a chance. As Larry Crabb suggests: "Abandon your demand to feel safe and make yourself available to be heard by another. Risk sharing your secrets with one friend. Risk telling your story and making known your struggles to a small group. It will backfire at times and you will have tales of verbal abuse. . . . But stay with it. To give up on soul-meeting community is to give up on life."[8]

SO HOW ABOUT YOU?

1. What stories do you have like these? In other words, what Isolation Games do you see other people playing (either ones listed in this chapter or others you can think of)? What Isolation Games do you play?

2. How often do you hold back saying something (or plan your comments before you say them), because you are concerned what others will think or say about your comments?

    a. Rarely

    b. Once per week

    c. Once per day

    d. More than once per day

3. What would life look like if you didn't play Isolation Games?

---

8. Ibid., 161–162.

MIDPOINT REVIEW

Wow! We are halfway through section 1, identifying the different types of games we play. We have already reviewed:

- ESP Games—how we speculate about another person's motives and feelings to protect ourselves from being hurt, and then we act on our speculations. We worked on asking what the other person is thinking or feeling—maybe by using reflective listening, or even just stating to that person what we are afraid he is thinking. We also discussed the more loving option of actually caring enough to get to know him and help him instead of speculating.

- Don't Change Me Games—how we feel threatened by losing control over our lives, so we exert the ultimate control and refuse to try to change. "It's my life and this is just the way I am," we say to ourselves. It's a way to avoid responsibility for future decisions or actions (even inaction). We miss seeing that change is inevitable, nothing is secure. We really can't change to become the composite person that everyone else wants us to be. So we discussed embracing change by asking God what to change in our lives.

- Avoiding Responsibility Games—how we try to avoid being accountable for our decisions and actions by blaming others and by going on the offensive. We even discussed how we act like we apologize, when we don't really mean to apologize at all. We identified the more loving option of just taking the responsibility and apologizing for our actions and decisions, while stating our fears to the other person (where we are afraid of the possible consequences of accepting the blame).

- Isolation Games—how some of us (especially introverts) play it safe with various Isolation Games, when we avoid disclosing our opinions and feelings to others. Then we discussed a couple of ways to open up—sharing three events from each day (including our feelings about those events) and sharing our stories with each other (stories from our past and our hopes and concerns about the future).

Maybe you have thought of other games you play to speculate rather than communicate, to avoid changing, to blame others rather than take responsibility, or to isolate yourself. Maybe you have even thought of other loving solutions to these games. If so, bravo! I am proud of you—I would cast my vote for you to stay in the lifeboat.

We still have four remaining types of relationship games to review—Be Perfect Like Me Games, Passive Be Like Me Games, Serve Me Games, and Looking Good Games. After those games, the fun really begins! In section 2 we will look at a major game changer, an attitude adjustment replacing these games with a more honest lifestyle. Then in section 3 we will spend some time investigating where God fits into our games and our relationships.

5

Be Perfect Like Me Games

I want you to benefit from my knowledge by influencing (even controlling) your attitudes and actions, so I protect my self-worth by pushing you to think and live like I do (with a Be Perfect Like Me Game). Instead of playing this game, I will humbly recognize I don't know it all and just ask you to consider my ideas.

LARRY CRABB DESCRIBES AN interview with a television reporter after two teenagers ruthlessly killed several classmates and a teacher at a high school in Columbine, Colorado:

> Reporter: What would make these young men do something so terrible? What does this say to us about the nature of evil and what we can do about it?
>
> Crabb: We'll not get far in understanding what went wrong with those young men until we recognize the same seed of evil in ourselves.... We'll speak of poor socialization, peer pressure, uninvolved parenting, genetic defect or the influence of media, music, and movies—anything but the radical self-centeredness that, except for Jesus, would keep all of us out of heaven.
>
> Reporter: [*stopping the camera and cutting the interview off suddenly*] I would never do what those boys did. I'm incapable of killing another human being.... Those two young men were evil in a way I'm not."[1]

---

1. Crabb, *Soul Talk*, 189–190.

The reporter (who ironically worked for a Christian network) was playing a Be Perfect Like Me Game, and it was no game to her. This was serious. In a way, this reporter was saying, "Why aren't these kids more like me? If they were like me, this would not have happened. As a matter of fact, if everyone was more like me, this world would be a better place." Gamers like this reporter think they have figured out the best way to think and live (at least in certain areas). They feel responsible to make your life (and their lives) better by convincing you to live the same way, and your refusal to agree strikes at the core of their identity and self-worth—their need to be right.

I have selected two examples of Be Perfect Like Me Games for our review:
- "What Were You Thinking?" Game
- "You Need to . . . " Game

PLAYING THE "WHAT WERE YOU THINKING?" GAME

Have you ever tried to talk logically to a teenager who doesn't see your point of view? He insists that you are clueless, and you think he is, too. You might as well be on different planets. You probably are on different planets. The conversation may have started because the teenager did something that seems so illogical to you. Before you could even think about it, you exclaimed in frustration, "What were you thinking?" You subconsciously wish he were more like you.

We do that to each other—not just to our teens. For example:
- An analyst at work sends a report out to a client that was not checked, and I find that the report has a major error in it. I react, "What were you thinking?"
- Beth backs our car into the basketball goal. I wonder, "What were you thinking?"
- I decide to wear a pair of wool pants to a spring family get-together. Beth exclaims, "What were you thinking?"

The interrogation begins. You hope for some logical answer to your question, but it never comes. After hearing the person's futile attempt to answer your question satisfactorily, you now wish he would have never tried to explain himself. Why didn't he just admit, "You know, I really wasn't [thinking]"? Those words of confession rarely surface. He really was thinking—just not like you think. Or, he made a human error (we are human, right?), so what he was thinking made sense at that moment.

Here is a personal example of the "What Were You Thinking?" Game. Beth is a very organized person. Before she takes on a new project, she likes her work area to be cleaned up with everything in its place. When we recently set aside a room beneath our deck to store tools and garden equipment, Beth was so excited. She enjoyed reorganizing our various tools. She went through cabinets and put similar items together. She labeled the containers. She bought some strips and hooks to hang up the larger tools. In the South, we say Beth was in "hog heaven."

As for me, I hate taking the time to organize stuff. I feel more comfortable seeing what I need to work on, so putting stuff away means I may never find it again. I can always think of something more important to do than to organize our stuff. While Beth delights in organizing, it feels like a waste of precious time to me.

Over the years, we have had our share of arguments, negotiations, and compromises over issues like this one. As we work through our differences, we each say under our breath, "What were you thinking?" Or, more clearly, "Can't you just be like me?"

To be even clearer: "Can't you have the same priorities that I have? I realize you can't be just like me, because you really are not as good as me in this area. But you could agree with me on what is important, and that would be good enough."

PLAYING THE "YOU NEED TO . . . "GAME"

Beth has a lot of practical knowledge. She majored in Home Economics/Interior Design in college, which certainly helps. Beth has also researched a lot of different topics and has come to the conclusion about the best approach to solving a lot of day-to-day issues. Our friends know about her expertise and call her frequently with questions about a variety of topics—a fun restaurant for a special dinner, how to get permanent marker out of a blouse, a really good recipe for whole-grain pasta, speeding up their computer, or possible next steps for a parent whose son is addicted to drugs.

In the earlier years of our marriage, I joked that:

- Beth was sometimes wrong but never in doubt;
- Beth should set up a toll phone number so she would get paid for all her advice—something like a toll number called 1-900-ASK-BETH;

- Beth needed a company to run. She reminded me of company presidents I knew. They are confident in their opinions and ready to convince others to follow their ideas.

People like Beth often play the "You Need to . . ." Game. Their goal is to improve life for everyone (especially themselves) and they have the answer(s). They are self-appointed advisors to their friends and family. They receive hand towels as gifts from their Just Kidding friends with the words, "I'm not bossy . . . I just have better ideas." Conversations with them go something like this:

- You are putting dishes in the dishwasher. The Be Perfect Like Me advisor comes over and coaches you on how to do this chore better. The advisor wisely counsels, "You need to put these dishes here because they don't get as clean when they are arranged your way." Then the advisor proceeds to explain the water flow in the dishwasher, which supports her instructions.
- A teenage son is working through the philosophical challenges of human free will and God's sovereignty. The advisor instructs, "You know, I worked through this issue a few years ago. You need to look at these passages in the Bible and you'll see that . . ."
- A friend is planning a trip to New York City. The advisor begins sharing the best way to see New York City, "Well, the first thing to do is to get your airplane tickets through this website. If you want to see a Broadway play, then you need to . . ."

Christians and other religious people can take the "You Need to" Game to another level, by playing the God Card. The God Card is like the Rook card. In the card game of Rook, the Rook trumps all the remaining cards and automatically takes the trick when it is played.

If God has spoken a certain way, then we want to align our lives with the way God has spoken. We also strongly believe that others should follow God's guidance as well, if they want to lead fulfilling lives. When I share how God has spoken to *me* about what *you* need to do, that is equivalent to me playing the God Card or the Rook card. My God-backed comments trump whatever thoughts or feelings you have.

Sometimes we make our case very obvious. "God told me that you need to . . ." or "the Bible says that you need to . . ." It's like playing the "You Need to . . ." Game on steroids. How can you argue with God and me? Whatever God says to me about you automatically trumps your ideas or possible decisions.

Finally, anyone can modify their "You Need to . . . " Game strategy with a little persistence—keep talking so you get the last word. When you disagree and don't want to follow my advice, I don't just give up. I am so intent on convincing you to be like me that I want the last word. Whatever you say, I am going to give you one last reason (or restate one of my previous reasons) to be like me. Of course, you would want to be like me, since this is my area of expertise. I just need to convince you to see the light, to see the error of your ways. Once you see all my points, of course you will then agree with me. At least that is what the typical Be Like Me Gamer believes.

Beth and one of our sons frequently tried to get in the last word in the "You Need to . . . " Games they played with each other. Beth recalls one such "discussion" in our kitchen. She doesn't remember the topic, but obviously they disagreed, and they both felt it was important enough to keep making one more point in the debate. The discussion, now heated into an argument, was going back and forth. Each one was trying to get in the last word. Beth had just made another point, obviously the clincher to convince our son that he was wrong and she was right. At this point, our son demonstrated his complete frustration by giving Beth the "finger" (or the "shooting her the bird," as some call it) and storming out of the kitchen. For those of you who like puns, you might say that our son had transformed the last word strategy into the last "bird" strategy.

> **BE PERFECT LIKE ME GAMERS WOULD RATHER BE RIGHT THAN BE REDEMPTIVE**
>
> When Karen Spears Zacharias describes members of the religion of Certainosity, she might as well be describing those who play Be Perfect Like Me Games. She compares them to cows:
>
>> Those wide-eyed creatures [cows] have 320-degree panoramic vision, enabling them to see in almost any direction. But that ability isn't worth a lick of beans when it comes to determining a threat. Cattle lack depth perception. They are frequently frightened by their own shadows. And since cattle are colorblind, their world is full of scary shadows.

> There are people [Be Perfect Like Me Gamers/followers of the religion of Certainosity] like that. People who believe they have the gift of panoramic vision who lack depth perception. Their entire world is black and white. They see terrifying shadows behind everything. . . . [While they feel threatened, these] disciples of Certainosity never question anything. They don't think they need to. Thanks to that gift of panoramic vision, they believe nothing escapes them. So these disciples don't have any doubts about themselves, about God, or about the word of God. . . . At its core, there's really no spiritual component to Certainosity. No mercy and certainly no grace . . .
>
> I know all about these people because I used to belong to the herd. I wasn't a bad or ignorant person. I simply thought I had a better view of the world than most outside the herd. We were a special breed of people, tagged and marked members of the religion of Certainosity. . . . foremost . . . was the belief that it's better to be right than redeemed.[2]
>
> Based on their desire to convert you to be like them, I prefer to change Zacharias's assessment slightly and say the Be Perfect Like Me Gamers would rather be right than be redemptive. No mercy, no healing, no reconciliation, unless you agree with them. Nothing to be redeemed in their lives—only the overwhelming desire to be right.

WHERE DO WE FEEL THREATENED? HOW DO WE TRY TO PROTECT OURSELVES WITH THESE GAMES?

At first, it is hard to believe the confident gamer who plays Be Perfect Like Me Games is threatened by anything. He is out to convert you to his point of view. Why would he need to protect himself?

From what Beth says, she was trying to deal with her subconscious fear that she would look stupid or be criticized. She also did not want to be misunderstood or be wrong. Her way of counteracting these threats was to research and come up with the best solutions for many of the important areas of her life—to become excellent (a perfectionist?) and to avoid being criticized. It was a lifeboat-type issue for her. What a good way to earn votes on the lifeboat—knowing more than other people and being a helpful resource fed her self-esteem. Who would then want to vote her off the lifeboat?

---

2. Zacharias, *Where's Your Jesus*, 71–72.

Be Perfect Like Me Gamers have a strong desire to control themselves and other people. They protect themselves from pain by controlling their lives as much as possible. They generally have a solution for some issue that I have, and they want me to adopt their solution. Obviously, if they have thought the issue through and they have come up with the best solution for them, it should be the best solution for me, too. They are afraid I won't adopt their solution, which may be painful to both of us.

Richard Foster offers this observation about those who want to convert others to be like themselves. "Pride takes over because we come to believe that we are the right kind of people. Fear takes over because we dread losing control. . . . We must come to the place in our lives where we can lay down the everlasting burden of always needing to manage others. . . . When we genuinely believe that inner transformation is God's work and not ours, we can put to rest our passion to set others straight."[3]

WHAT ARE THE UNINTENDED MESSAGES WE ARE SENDING?

Have you noticed that the name of this game—the Be Perfect Like Me Game—has a Mary Poppins sound to it? You know, practically perfect in every way. I think this is the way most of these gamers see themselves—kind and helpful, like Mary Poppins. They think their concern to help others make the best decisions possible (= the decisions they would make) is a giving way to live. It is hard to believe, but even the most God-seeking Be Perfect Like Me Gamers can become obviously manipulative when they are trying to get others to follow them (= follow God). Manipulation becomes a necessary, even helpful part of the process to lead others to honor God. Ironically, this approach doesn't honor God's ability to work in their lives without our schemes to help God out.

Secondly, the "in-your-face" advisor who plays Be Perfect Like Me Games often sends the unintended message that the other person is stupid. Initially, the advisor comes across as helpful, but as he goes on and on, he comes across as domineering and arrogant, instead of helpful. In his effort to be helpful and convincing, he implies that the other person is helpless and cannot think for herself. The Be Perfect Like Me Gamer

---

3. Foster, *Celebration*, 10.

does not trust others to make decisions without his advice. Think about how that feels to the one receiving the advice.

When someone plays Be Like Me Games, he has a heavy burden to bear. He needs to be right almost all the time. This means he tends to ignore the inconsistencies in his own life—when he violates his own principles. Thus, he comes across as hypocritical when he ignores the times he doesn't live up to his well-vocalized standards.

WHAT ARE SOME LOVING SOLUTIONS TO REPLACE THESE GAMES?

Over the past few years, Beth and I have gone through some gut-wrenching times together. Since then, Beth has become less interested in convincing others that her opinion is the best one—the one we all should adopt so that our lives would be better. So she doesn't play the "You Need to . . . " or other Be Perfect Like Me Games as much anymore. In Beth's words, "My personal trials held a mirror up to my face, and I didn't like the self-righteous, know-it-all person I saw in the mirror. I began to realize that I didn't know as much as I thought. I recognized God may be leading other people on a different journey than mine, and that was okay."

Larry Crabb longs for us Be Like Me Gamers to experience a similar transformation—"ongoing seasons of pride-shattering brokenness" that "arouse [our] appetite for God" and authentic relationships. Until we "see the tangled mess of perverted, self-obsessed desires that drive so much of what we think and feel and do,"[4] we will continue to play the Be Perfect Like Me Games. Once we admit our underlying selfish, manipulative, game-playing desires, we are less likely to insist that others should be like us.

If I were reading this book, I would now be thinking:

Reader: Thanks for sharing some of Beth's personal trials. I see she is working on being more transparent. Are you saying I have to go through some type of suffering to stop playing Be Perfect Like Me Games?

Joe: I can't say what God will do in your life. It seems the key issue is to replace arrogance with humility. You need to recognize that your opinions, personality traits, decision-making processes, etc.,

---

4. Crabb, *Real Church*, 44–46.

are not necessarily the best ones for everybody else. They may not even be the best ones for you.

Reader: Thank you, Captain Obvious. By the way, are you playing the "You Need to . . . " Game while telling me how to avoid playing the "You Need to . . . " Game?

Joe: [*ignoring the question, as I sometimes do when someone points out an inconsistency in my life*] Actually, I wasn't finished being obvious. Once you no longer have to prove your ideas are the best ones, you can be more patient with others who don't agree with you. You can also more readily see and admit your personal challenges, replacing hypocrisy with a more realistic self-image.

Reader: Okay. Do you have anything that is not so obvious?

Joe: [*in a statement of apparent humility*] Maybe this is obvious, too. Watch out when you are feeling superior to someone else. Or when you are feeling frustrated by another person's illogical thinking or actions. Or when you feel threatened that the other person is making you look stupid or wrong. All those are warning signs that you are playing a Be Perfect Like Me Game.

Let's look at some examples. Remember the reporter who was interviewing Larry Crabb about the Columbine murderers? Remember how she said she could never be like them, because she would never kill anyone? When that thought goes through your mind and you get that feeling of superiority, ask yourself (or ask God) how you actually resemble that person you are judging. Or at least think like that person. In this example, how do you act in a murderous way toward other people, even if you don't commit the act of murder? Is your backbiting a type of verbal murder? Do you wish someone was dead, even though you haven't actually killed him?

Consider another example. You frequently see a relative high and/or drunk. She is unable to keep a job, and she is ignoring her husband and her children. Your first thought is, "I am so disappointed in her. She was not raised this way. I could never do to my family what she is doing to them." In this case, you think she is medicating some pain with her drug/alcohol use. So you ask yourself, "How do I medicate my life against pain?" Maybe your method of avoiding pain is to run off to work where decisions are not so messy. Your method is legal. Is it really any different? Are you really facing up to your personal challenges and learning through your pain, or are you just medicating your pain in a different way?

These are humbling questions that reveal our own inadequacies. We really aren't better than they are—our self-focused approach may just be more socially acceptable. The world really wouldn't be better if everyone was like us.

So let's stop beating ourselves up about our arrogance and look at the flip side. Letting go of the need to be right all the time is actually a freeing way to live. In my experience, I have much less to protect in my life if I don't have to be right. I can just admit when I make mistakes. It's okay. I am human. Not only am I freed from my need to be right, but I'm also freed from my need to transform others to be like me. I can trust God to transform them as he sees fit. It's not up to me.

I then experience the magnitude of God's undeserved, irrational kindness as I see all the areas in my life where I fall short of loving God and other people. I actually see that if others try to be like me, they may not be that much better off. Maybe I'm not practically perfect after all. Going a step further, I recognize that God is so good and gracious to keep loving me unconditionally, in spite of myself. Lord, give me the strength to love myself and others like you love me.

Once I come to this point of view, I am ready to apply Dallas Willard's suggestion for all Be Perfect Like Me Gamers, which he calls "the dynamic of *the request*":

> As long as I am condemning my friends or relatives, or pushing my "pearls" [of wisdom] on them, I am their problem. They have to respond to me, and that usually leads to their "judging" me right back....
>
> But once I back away, maintaining a sensitive and nonmanipulative presence, I am no longer their problem. As I listen, they do not have to protect themselves from me, and they begin to open up. I may quickly begin to appear to them as a possible ally and resource. Now they begin to see their problem as the situation they have created, or possibly themselves. Because I am no longer trying to drive them, genuine communication, real sharing of hearts, becomes an attractive possibility. The healing dynamic of the request comes naturally into play....
>
> Our approach to influencing others, for their good as well as ours, will be simply *to ask*: to ask them to change, and to help them in any way they ask of us.[5]

---

5. Willard, *Divine Conspiracy*, 231–232.

As Gary Chapman puts it, "Requests give direction to love, but demands stop the flow of love."[6] I want my communications with others to promote a loving relationship, more than trying to control them with my views of the world. I want to be redemptive more than I want to be right.

So instead of insisting we are right, we recognize we may be off base somewhere, too. Instead of judging, we try to duplicate God's love for us (in spite of our own failures). Instead of condemning, we listen. Instead of demanding, we ask.

> **LOGICALLY, USING LOGIC IS THE BEST WAY TO MAKE DECISIONS**
>
> Most of the time, I am a logical, unemotional guy. So when I make decisions, it is natural for me to make those decisions logically. I naturally assume that emotions can't be trusted, because they may lead me to make an illogical decision. I have seen some people make some really poor decisions when they responded emotionally.
>
> That was my view of the world. It was generally reinforced by my parents and by my wife and our sons. Each one of us made decisions based on logic, until our third son came along. Guess what? He was more comfortable making decisions based on how he felt. In my view, his decision-making process was not as reliable. Logically, using logic is the best way to make decisions, so I tried to teach our youngest son how to change his decision process. I was not very successful.
>
> During some family counseling we were questioning many of our assumptions. This one came to my mind—my assumption that making decisions logically is better than making decisions based on feelings. We have a friend whose son makes his decisions based on his feelings. In the middle of the night, he felt led by God to a bridge, where he talked a man out of committing suicide. And the man could not speak any English! Our friend's son was also led to a "chance" meeting with Madonna, to tell her that she was God's beloved. This young man made these illogical and loving decisions based on his feelings (his openness to God). I doubt that I would

---

6. Chapman, *Five Love Languages*, 92.

> ever have been so open to God's spirit to do these "crazy" acts of love. They just don't make sense to me—I am too logical.
>
> Another wake-up call for me: I no longer believe that making decisions based on logic is the best approach. Making decisions based on God's leading (whether through logic or feelings) leads to the best decisions. My youngest son (or anyone else) does not have to make decisions logically like me to function well in his life.

WHAT ARE SOME POSITIVE ASPECTS OF THESE GAMES?

Helping others avoid issues or solve problems is a noble calling. At least I think so, since that is what I do as an employee-benefit consultant. Beth, the other leaders, and I also try to help parents in our support group deal with their family issues, which we have already encountered in our own lives. This book is intended to help you with your relationship issues. In a sense, I am using our experience to teach others how to be like me sometimes, when I am not playing these games. Even the New Testament writer, the Apostle Paul, encouraged his readers in several of his letters to follow his example in making God-based decisions (1 Cor 4:16, Gal 4:12, Phil 3:17).

So what's the difference? I have identified some Be Perfect Like Me Games that hinder positive relationships, while the above examples illustrate times when we teach others to learn from us—maybe even be like us.

When I play a Be Perfect Like Me Game, I believe that you should be thinking/acting like I do—according to my standards. I am annoyed by our differences that may be causing some problems for me in my life. I lose patience and feel offended if you don't take my advice or live by my priorities. I even feel responsible for "straightening you out," because I believe you will be miserable until you change to become like me. Instead of listening to you and working together to brainstorm the best solution to help you, I already have the solution (typically a formula that has worked for me) and I am trying to fit my solution to your problem. My identity depends on my ability to convince you to be like me. I am thinking/acting in an arrogant and controlling manner.

Dallas Willard puts it this way: "Condemnation, especially with its usual accompaniment of anger and contempt and self-righteousness, blinds us to the reality of the other person. We cannot 'see clearly' how to assist our brother, because we cannot see our brother. And we will never know how to truly help him until we have grown into the kind of person who does not condemn."[7]

On the other hand, when I am truly being helpful, I listen to your feelings and ideas. We can brainstorm possible solutions, without me feeling that you must follow my advice. Even if I feel strongly that you are making harmful choices, I am patient. I am comfortable letting you walk the journey you have chosen, trusting God to work in you as God continues to work in me. I can share what I believe God says about this topic, while giving you the freedom to disagree. I recognize we are each still a work in progress. I don't have a formula solution; instead, I can share how I have worked through a similar problem before and just see if that idea might work for you. My identity depends on my relationship to God and his purpose for my life, not on your willingness to follow my will for your life. I am thinking/acting with patience, humility, and empathy.

> ### How You Say It Is Important—Your Attitude Is Critical
>
> In our parenting-support group, we have developed a list of phrases to avoid using when talking to our teenage and adult children. We have also come up with alternative phrases to use. Our goal is to be able to give advice to our children while honoring their freedom to make their own choices. The same point seems to apply here—how you say it can show whether you are playing Be Perfect Like Me Games or trying to be authentically helpful:
>
> | Phrases to Avoid | Phrases to Use |
> |---|---|
> | What were you thinking? | Will you help me understand? |
> | You need to . . . | When I was in a similar situation I . . . |
> | Why would you . . . ? | In my view of the world, I would . . . |
> | What is wrong with you? | So what I hear you saying is . . . |
> | The Bible says you should . . . | The way I interpret the Bible, I would . . . |
> | Let me tell you how to do this . . . | How do you think I can help you? Would you be interested in my thoughts? If I were you, I would consider . . . |

---

7. Willard, *Divine Conspiracy*, 224.

> If you can replace the Phrases to Avoid with the Phrases to Use, you can ensure your speech matches up with your intention to be helpful. Of course, using the right phrases while still trying to control the other person is still a game.
>
> You know, I think I can turn any helpful strategy like this into a relationship game if my attitude is off base. Lord, when I think of my own tendency to judge others, to want to make them like me, all I can do is pray for you to transform my attitude. Help me really care enough to stop trying to control my friends and family!

SO HOW ABOUT YOU?

1. What stories do you have like these? In other words, what Be Perfect Like Me Games do you see other people playing (either ones listed in this chapter or others you can think of)? What Be Perfect Like Me Games do you play?

2. It seems obvious—Be Perfect Like Me Gamers rarely believe they are wrong. How often do you conclude you are wrong in your opinions or statements or actions?

    a. I rarely ever admit I am wrong

    b. Once per week

    c. Once per day

    d. More than once per day

3. Since Be Perfect Like Me Gamers tend to think they have it all figured out, they often give others advice, even when the other people haven't asked for it. So how about you—how often do you give others unsolicited advice?

    a. I rarely ever give others unsolicited advice.

    b. Once per week

    c. Once per day

    d. More than once per day

4. What would life look like if you didn't play Be Perfect Like Me Games?

6

Passive Be Like Me Games

I want to prove that I am better than you without dealing with the conflict of convincing you to change, so I protect my self-worth by judging and criticizing you in a passive way (with a Passive Be Like Me Game). Instead of playing this game, I will recognize I don't know it all and listen and empathize with you, and, if needed, confront you with humility.

I CONFESS THAT MY friends and I have played the ESP Game about others' motives. (Of course, that was before we read the loving solutions to the ESP Game in chapter 1.) When someone appears to manipulate a situation to get what they want in a sneaky, not-so-obvious way, we say, "Wow! Wasn't she passive-aggressive?"

Based on that experience, I had initially identified some of these Be Like Me Games as passive-aggressive. Then I decided to look up the clinical definition of "passive-aggressive." According to the American Psychiatric Association, a person with a passive-aggressive personality has four or more of the following characteristics:

- Resists fulfilling routine social and occupational tasks
- Complains of being misunderstood and unappreciated by others
- Is sullen and argumentative
- Unreasonably criticizes and scorns authority
- Expresses envy and resentment toward those apparently more fortunate

- Voices exaggerated and persistent complaints of personal misfortune
- Alternates between hostile defiance and contrition.[1]

Wow! To be passive-aggressive, a person has to exhibit at least four of these seven characteristics. There is a lot more to being "passive-aggressive" than I thought. I drew two conclusions from my research:

- Here is *another* example of the problems with the ESP Game. Not only do I not really know someone's motives, in this case I don't even understand what it really means to be passive-aggressive.
- If you understood all the aspects of being passive-aggressive, when would you admit to playing passive-aggressive games? So I decided to change the title of this chapter to Passive Be Like Me Games.

When I initially categorized several games as Be Like Me Games, I recognized that I played similar games in a more subtle fashion. I still wanted others to be like me, but I wasn't willing to be that obvious about it. Beth may be the star of the more obvious Be Perfect Like Me Games in chapter 5, but I am the poster child for the Passive Be Like Me Games in chapter 6. I still share my opinion about the best solution for another person's problem, just phrased differently. I wonder if my subtle approaches come across any better. My guess is the more strongly I feel about my proposed solution, the more it comes across as "you need to . . . ," whether I use those words or not.

Remember the Be Perfect Like Me sign, "I'm not bossy—I just have better ideas." We have that sign in one of our bedrooms (obviously a gift to Beth). This is exactly opposite of how I want to come across to my friends and family. I don't want to appear bossy or a know-it-all. That's why the Passive Be Like Me Games work so well for me—I think I can more subtly make my point with these games.

Here are two examples of Passive Be Like Me Games

- Masked Judgment Game
- Just Kidding Game

---

1. Ward, Deborah, "Passive-Aggressive Personality."

PLAYING THE MASKED JUDGMENT GAME

We all agree that gossip is not a loving form of communication. It is passive, because we are not interacting with the person involved. Sometimes, we spread a rumor (or possibly even a fact) while masking our gossip and judgment through various Masked Judgment Games. We wish these people were more like us, but we don't have the guts to confront them directly, so we use a more passive approach with these games.

For example, Susan has an unmarried, teenage daughter named Meg. Meg just found out that she is pregnant, presumably not on purpose. The Masked Judgment Game can be played in various ways at this point:

- The Bless Her Heart Approach: "Did you hear about Meg getting pregnant? I heard she stopped taking the pill. She never was very smart—bless her heart." This is a common method in the South of masking gossip. We can add "bless his/her heart" to the end of any piece of gossip and rationalize that we are not guilty of judging or gossiping

- The Pray for Her Approach: "Did you hear? We really need to pray for Susan's family. Meg just found out she is pregnant. I bet Susan is so embarrassed. Who was Meg dating anyway?" Instead of adding "bless her heart," we mask our judgment with their need for prayer.

- The You Need to Know Approach: "Have you talked to your teenager about the dangers of premarital sex? You need to know this about Susan, because it will convince you to talk to your teenager again. I heard Susan's daughter got pregnant. Her physician prescribed birth-control pills for Meg, and Susan didn't even know about it. Then I heard Meg stopped taking the pill and now she is [*pausing for emphasis*] with child."

- The He/She Deserves It Approach: "You know how Susan always struts around, telling all of us how to raise our children. Even last month she was pointing out how well Meg was doing in school and soccer. She was the model child. Well, you won't believe this—Meg is pregnant. We probably won't hear much from Susan for a while."

Sometimes we use feeling hurt to mask our judgment of others. If I have been hurt, I somehow feel more justified in my judgment of someone else. For example, I invited my wife's co-workers, along with our friends, to a special birthday party for my wife. Our friends came, but no one from work came to the party. Actually, none of them even let me know they weren't coming—of course, I did just send an e-mail invite. Well, they did take her to lunch to celebrate her special day. All that is irrelevant, as I shared with my son how thoughtless my wife's co-workers were—to not come or even RSVP. How could they be so inconsiderate! Of course, if I had been in their shoes, I would have sent an RSVP. Why don't they think like me? They must not care (a little ESP Game going on, too).

A slight variation on the Masked Judgment Game is to mask your judgment with silence. My mama always told me, "Joe, if you don't have something nice to say about someone, just don't say anything at all." Instead of expressing my judgments to others, I just say them to myself. I am still judging others. As I recall what Jesus said at the Sermon on the Mount, my attitudes (thoughts) are what really matter. So being judgmental without speaking judgmentally still seems to be a Passive Be Like Me Game. I am not confronting the issue—my attitude of superiority. I am still saying (in my mind), "Why can't you be like me?"

> **THE MASKED JUDGMENT GAME AT WORK**
>
> I frequently see people using the You Need to Know Approach and the He/She Deserves It Approach at work. Of course, the topic is typically not a pregnancy, but it could be. The You Need to Know Approach is the more subtle one. To justify using the You Need to Know Approach, the gossiper has to come up with a reason the hearer needs to know this rumor/fact. It could help the hearer do a better job, get hired, not get fired, land a new client, etc. The hearer will probably benefit in some way, so that means it is okay (even helpful) to share this gossip. Of course, the gossiper must benefit in some way. Maybe it increases his sense of importance or puts him in a more favorable light. The judgment is masked or at least justified. For example:
>
> Juan: Don't you work with Ralph on some of his accounts? You better be prepared—I am not sure Ralph will be around much lon-

ger. You'll end up with even more work than you have now. Maybe you'll get promoted, too.

April: What are you talking about?

Juan: I heard that some people are being laid off and Ralph's blunder with the McKenzie account may cost him his job. Here's what happened . . .

More subtly, we can use a co-worker's poor performance as a reason to let his boss in on the issue, without talking directly to the employee first. We rationalize this approach by saying it is really the manager's responsibility to deal with the co-worker's performance, not ours. In this case, we are taking the easy way out by not "giving the employee the benefit of the doubt and checking it out" directly with him first. A lot of misunderstandings could be resolved if we went directly to the employee before talking to his manager. You know, our observations and ESP assumptions may be wrong.

Often, the He/She Really Deserves It Approach starts with our perception that the other person has hurt us intentionally. The quality of our work or our integrity has been questioned. Admitting a mistake feels "career-threatening," so we not only play the Blame Game, but we also spread facts/rumors about the person who is "trying to get us." It can feel like a life-or-death matter. In a sense, we are being voted off the lifeboat, all because of this simple mistake (or implication of a mistake). Thus, we need to defend and protect ourselves.

When we play the Masked Judgment Game, we don't confront the co-worker or issue directly. Instead, we backbite and bring up problems this person has in some behind-the-scenes conversations. We tell events that cause others to question this person's work or integrity. And we justify our actions because he deserves it.

Here is some irony. If you are like me, I would be offended if someone did the same thing to me. "Why didn't he just come directly to me with his concerns?" I innocently ask myself. Probably because he is playing the same Masked Judgment Game that I have been playing.

PLAYING THE JUST KIDDING GAME

Males seem to frequently play the Just Kidding Game—it seems to match their strengths. Guys often prefer this game in a group, even though the verbal interchange often occurs between two guys. One male has a negative message to deliver to another guy. He may have already played the ESP Game and the Masked Judgment Game with some others in the group, to make sure they agree with his opinion. Rather than do this one-on-one in private, the one with the message prefers to deliver the message in front of the group as a joke.

For example, four guys (Bob, Jim, Mike, and Ron) are playing a round of golf. Bob is not playing well and he is getting frustrated. He just hit another poor tee shot, this one into the woods, so Jim decides to add to Bob's misery. Who knows why? Maybe in some way Bob does not fit Jim's idea of what a man should be like. Bob obviously isn't like Jim.

> Jim: You know, Bob, I don't see how you play golf with those old golf clubs anyway. Look at your driver. Playing with that old driver is like drag racing with a moped. You've got no chance. [*Everyone in the group chuckles. I'm not sure why—it wasn't that funny. Anyway, everyone in the group knows Bob plays with old, "ratty-looking" clubs. They really are old, and it is hard not to notice.*]
>
> Bob: [*sarcastically*] Thanks for the suggestion, Jim. I'm sure your idea is going to help me today. [*Humor begets humor.*]
>
> Jim: Well, I'm just trying to help you out for the next time. Wearing that sissy pink shirt can't help you, either.
>
> Ron: [*trying to deflect the criticism without seeming disloyal to either Jim or Bob*] Bob, how old is that driver anyway. Is it a Wilson Staff? You might actually get a good offer on eBay for that classic.
>
> Jim: [*ignoring Ron's attempt*] I bet your pink shirt is attracting the golf ranger, too. He can see us a mile away. I give you ten-to-one odds that he comes back soon and tells us to speed up our play . . . again. Do you think we have time to look for your ball in the woods? It went way right.
>
> Ron: Hey, Jim, cut Bob some slack. He's just having a bad day.
>
> Jim: Come on, Ron. I was just kidding. We all have our bad days, don't we Bob? I know I've had one or two myself.

What do you think Jim's real message is? It is actually hard to tell. For example:

- Jim could be tired of helping Bob look for his lost golf balls.
- Jim could be irritated and embarrassed that the golf ranger keeps getting on the group to speed up their play, and he thinks the solution is for Bob to stop looking for the balls he hits into the woods.
- Jim could be frustrated that Bob's poor play is messing up Jim's concentration and score. If Bob sped up, Jim would play better.
- He may just be feeling superior to Bob and letting him know it—right now Jim is safely in the lifeboat because Bob is not, at least not based on Bob's old golf clubs or today's golf game. Jim is even earning more approval from the group by cracking jokes about Bob's play.

Whatever his message, he is delivering it passively and using humor to mask his attack. When Jim is called out on his attack by Ron, he drops back to the "just kidding" line so he does not need to explain himself. Jim then adds some empathy for Bob's bad day, which no one knows how to take. Is Jim still "just kidding" that everyone has bad days, or is he implying that Bob has a lot more than one or two bad days?

Who knows? Who will ever know, as long as we dance around our messages with subtle humor? Using humor in this way just reinforces the need to play the ESP Game to guess the real message. How will we ever communicate what we really mean if we play games that force us to play other games?

SARCASM OR DRY WIT?

Our immediate family is known for its dry wit. Beth, each of our three sons, and I can each tease each other (or other people) with our sarcasm. We call it "giving them a hard time." Sarcasm is typically part of the Just Kidding Game. We use it to point out some inconsistency (something stupid or selfish, for example) in the other person's speech or actions. And we do it in a humorous manner. While funny, sarcasm can be downright cruel. As one friend told me lately, "Joe, you are a nice guy, except when you are trying to be funny." Bingo! He hit that nail on the head!

> Brent, our middle son, pointed out recently that we tend to criticize someone for being sarcastic, but we praise someone who has a dry wit. Dry wit is typically considered a higher form of humor. He wondered why, since they are basically the same. I decided to compare their definitions:
>
> - **Sarcasm:** a sharp and often satirical or ironic utterance designed to cut or give pain [or] a mode of satirical wit depending for its effect on bitter, caustic, and often ironic language that is usually directed against an individual.[2]
>
> - **Dry Wit:** The ability to criticize someone and have them laugh about it . . . [or] Humor that soars over the heads of your less-intellectual friends.[3]
>
> I think I figured it out (which earns me a seat in the lifeboat, right?). Those who use dry wit think of themselves as smarter than other people, because only more "intelligent" people recognize the humor. It now makes sense. Dry wit feeds the pride of the jokester and his audience. Some kinder people would recognize my words as cruel sarcasm and would disapprove (vote me off the lifeboat), but others would laugh along with me at the irony of the joke. It is in their best interest to laugh along. By understanding the joke and laughing at it, they are automatically putting themselves in the smaller, respected group of "intelligent" people who get it.
>
> What a perfect set-up! I tell a critical joke with "dry wit" and you need to laugh to prove you are smart enough to get it. You can't afford not to laugh, even if it isn't funny. To not laugh equates to not being smart enough to understand the joke, and stupid people get voted off the lifeboat. (Maybe that's why Bob's friends laughed at Jim's sarcastic/dry wit joke—to stay in the intelligence lifeboat.)

---

2. Merriam-Webster Dictionary, s.v. "sarcasm," accessed May 17, 2011. Online: http://www.merriam-webster.com/dictionary/sarcasm.

3. Urban Dictionary, s.v. "dry wit," accessed May 17, 2011. Online: http://www.urbandictionary.com/define.php?term=dry%20wit.

WHERE DO WE FEEL THREATENED? HOW DO WE TRY TO PROTECT OURSELVES WITH THESE GAMES?

Unlike people who play the Be Perfect Like Me Games, the Passive Be Like Me Gamer is not willing to confront others directly with his suggestions for improvement (judgments). When I play the Passive Be Like Me Games, I still want others to change and be like me—I just don't want to appear to be controlling. I actually make fun of those who are obviously so controlling (using the Just Kidding Game).

So what am I trying to protect myself from? Here are some possibilities:

- I really don't like conflict, but I do wish you were more like me. I think if you were more like me (or at least more like my vision of myself), my life (and maybe yours) would be better. So how do I get that message across to you, without dealing with the potential pain of conflict? I play the Just Kidding Game or one of the Judgment Games, hoping you eventually get the message. I just don't have the guts to confront you directly with my "suggestions for improvement."

- I may also be avoiding confrontation because I really don't want my values and opinions to be challenged. I don't want the conflict of a debate over my judgment of you, because you might try to prove me wrong. Instead, I hang around people who think like me, where my opinions won't be challenged. Then we can be so agreeable in our arrogant judgment of others.

- I want you to respect me and accept me. In essence, I am protecting myself from getting voted off the lifeboat. One way to meet this goal is for me to look good, which leads to me playing a Looking Good Game (coming soon to a chapter near you). Or, I can just make someone else look worse than me, using one of the Masked Judgment Games. I use my own internal standards to judge that person, showing how he is not behaving the right way (= the way I would do it). As long as I bring down someone else to a lower level than me, all the criticism focuses on that person, not on me. The pressure is off me. I am safely in the lifeboat . . . for now.

So what is going on within me when I silently play the Masked Judgment Game? As weird as it sounds, I am trying to justify why I don't vote myself off the lifeboat. I need to believe I am better than someone else, to avoid the self-criticism I would otherwise direct at myself. Therapists say that a person who is very critical of other people is also just as critical of himself, so it should be no surprise that I have to justify my superiority, even proving it to myself. Again, if I am criticizing/judging someone else, the internal pressure is off my own self-criticism . . . for now.

WHAT ARE THE UNINTENDED MESSAGES WE ARE SENDING?

By playing Passive Be Like Me Games, I don't want to appear controlling or like a "know–it–all." Assuming I am successful in masking my real intentions, I still end up looking judgmental—judgmental in a sarcastic or backbiting manner. I probably end up looking judgmental, because I am judgmental. I am just as judgmental as the "in-your-face" Be Perfect Like Me advisor from chapter 5.

The trade-off doesn't sound that good. Instead of looking controlling or proud, I send you the message that I am critical and judgmental. I may get some positive votes for my dry wit, but I am never sure that those dry-wit votes are enough to keep me in the lifeboat.

Some people actually see through my Passive Be Like Me Games. They also get the message that I am trying to control them while trying to avoid conflict. Even if I am masking my judgment with silence, the tone of my voice and my body language can give my thoughts and attitudes away.

WHAT ARE SOME LOVING SOLUTIONS TO REPLACE THESE GAMES?

It seems rather simple. If you have a message to give to someone else, don't hide it behind humor and don't go tell other people. Go directly to the person, speak your message as clearly and lovingly as you can, and recognize your own inadequacies while planning your conversation. If the message could be taken critically, you may want to use the "sandwich approach." Sandwich your potentially negative comment between two positive ones. For example:

> Project Manager: [*trying to be caring while holding the employee accountable*] I just got a call from Jane at ABC Company. She is really frustrated by how late we are on their project. Her boss is mad and embarrassed that the Board of Directors doesn't have our report yet.

You know, this is really not like you, to be late with your work [*the first positive comment*]. What is going on, from your perspective?

Employee: [*playing the Blame Game*] Jane sent their information to us late, and it has put us behind. If she had been on time, we would have gotten the report done on time.

Project Manager: Anything else?

Employee: [*now using the Going on the Defensive Game*] I had two other projects going on at the same time. I worked late the last couple of days, but I just couldn't get it all done.

Project Manager: First things first—who else here can help you with ABC Company? And with help, how much longer will it take to finish this project? Second, for the future, you need to let your supervisor and me know if you are running behind on a project. You can't wait until the client calls with a problem to let me know something is wrong [*the negative feedback, in the middle*]. I think you and the rest of our team have what it takes to pull this off [*the second positive comment*].

Notice how the project manager went directly to the employee, instead of playing a Passive Be Like Me Game of griping to others in the office about the employee. In this case, he went directly to the employee to figure out the issue. He didn't use sarcasm to make his point. He also avoided the temptation to play Be Perfect Like Me Game and say, "What were you thinking?"

This type of upfront, honest, loving feedback isn't easy. Obviously, if this had been the second or third time the employee had not notified the project manager about a late project, the project manager may not have had the positive comments to use in the "sandwich." There is no magic formula. Ask God to give you wisdom and humility through the entire feedback process.

Some Passive Be Like Me Gamers also have similar challenges to those who play the in-your-face Be Like Me Games in chapter 5. They feel superior to others, have judgmental attitudes, and want to (more subtly) try to convert you to their point of view. When I have these attitudes, the same loving solutions from chapter 5 are available to me:

- Recognize that I don't really know it all
- Recognize that I also have personal faults that may be just as harmful as those obvious ones I see in that other person

- Recognize that my solutions may not work for someone else—God may have her on a different journey than me

Others who play Passive Be Like Me Games are trying to prove themselves as worthy of acceptance and even praise. These are lifeboat issues—looking to someone else or even myself to tell me I am valuable. Stop acting superior. We are not really better than those we are judging.

The loving (even freeing) alternative is to look to God to validate your worth. Let him guide your thoughts and actions to love others. Stop looking for approval from others. Set forth to love others and don't worry about what other people will say about you. The lifeboat is a myth! You don't need their votes to really live.

Finally, I find I am more understanding, more empathetic, and less judgmental of a person when I know his story. What has his life been like? How did he get to where he is today—the struggles and the victories? Instead of judging, I can be a safe place for that person to share himself with me, and I can watch while God works in my life to share with him what God has taught me—not out of a desire to make God work the same way in his life but out of my yearning to see how God will work in his life, too.

I can take my attempt at empathy a step further when I realize that if I had lived that person's life with his genetic make-up, I could actually be that person. I don't even have to know his story to recognize that I might be making the very same decisions he is making. With his background, I could be just like him, making apparently illogical or inconsiderate decisions. Then I can go one more step and realize that I am like him, that even with my own genes and life experiences, I make some similar illogical and inconsiderate decisions. They may look different in some ways, but I am just as guilty in my heart of the same poor motives or decisions, the ones leading me to judge him before I had this little epiphany about myself.

If I could be like him or I really am like him, my Be Like Me judgments fall away. They lose their power over me. That's great! I really don't want to live in that judgmental place, anyway.

> **WATCH OUT FOR THAT SMUG FEELING**
>
> Recently, a co-worker Linda and I had an early morning airplane flight to Newark, New Jersey. Linda was ahead of me in the security line. I had fallen behind a slow-moving, older woman. I was

watching as the older woman tried to figure out how to manage the security procedures. I was saying to myself, "It's okay. Take a deep breath. I am in no rush. I will be patient." (I never thought about offering to help the older woman navigate the security process. I was too busy being patient to think about being helpful.)

She was putting her stuff in a security bin, while I was taking off my shoes and belt, unloading my laptop computer, and so on. Just as I thought might happen, she then tried to go through the scanner with her coat on, so the security guard had to send her back, while asking her to remove her coat. I was watching all this in front of me and pushing my bins toward the scanning machine, when a woman behind me spoke up, "Excuse me, sir."

"Is she talking to me?" I asked myself. Then I turned around and a younger lady was talking to me. "You left your shoes on the floor back here," she said politely.

Sure enough, I had taken off my shoes and not put them in the security bin. They were on the floor at the woman's feet. Slightly embarrassed, I walked back to get them. To hide the embarrassment, I tried to say something funny, "Thanks. I hope to wake up by the time my flight lands in New Jersey." I smiled sheepishly, grabbed my shoes, and put them in one of my security bins. This event really didn't slow anyone down, because that older lady was still fumbling with her coat. My absent-mindedness with my shoes had not held anyone up, not really. No need to be embarrassed. I had recovered with a little humor.

Looking back on the situation, I was still feeling safe in the lifeboat. Since she was holding up the line, the older lady could possibly be voted off the lifeboat, bless her heart. But not me. (Beth later helped me sort out my feelings at this point. I was feeling smug.)

After taking off her coat and putting it in the bin, the older woman shuffled through the body scanner. I politely (smugly) waited my turn and then walked through the scanner with no problem. I waited patiently (although not helpfully) as she gathered her coat and put it on. My stuff was now coming through the luggage scanner, and I grabbed my stuff and walked gingerly out of the security area toward Linda. As I was repacking my computer, I looked up and noticed that the same younger woman who had reminded me about my shoes was walking toward me. Before I had time to wonder why she had walked forty feet out of the security area to see me, she politely said, "Excuse me, sir. You left your carry-on luggage on the security belt."

Sure enough, I had everything with me, except my carry-on luggage bag. I again attempted to recover with a little humor, as I walked back to get my luggage. "Thanks again," I said as I nodded my head to her. "It must be early signs of dementia." When our eyes met as we passed, she seemed to have this look of sincere pity in her eyes. She was probably concerned whether I would even make it to my destination without her help (using my ESP). Then I had this epiphany, presumably from God:

- I had been silently playing the Masked Judgment Game with the older lady in front of me. Why couldn't she be more like me and navigate these security lines like the traveling professional that I am? Feeling smug and overconfident, I had looked down on her. I had masked my arrogance and pride with my attempts at patience. I didn't even notice I was playing this game at the time, since I was too busy patting myself on the back for being patient.

- I chuckled at the irony. While I was feeling sorry for this lady, bless her heart, I actually had more problems in the security line than she did. The woman behind me, who was being patient *and* helpful to me, had more justifiable reasons to wonder if I could make it through the day. My chuckling turned to sorrow. What a lesson in humility! God, help me! I really do need to be saved from myself and my pride.

- Plus, I made a note for the future: Watch out when I am feeling smug! It is a warning sign from God that I could be arrogantly playing one of the Be Like Me Games. Maybe I should look for a way to instead be patient, humble, *and* helpful the next time I get this smug feeling.[4]

---

4. Maybe I could reorient my attitude, like Jan Johnson. In her words, "I [now] go to the airport to help people (not merely to fly), especially older people. If I see someone drop something, I pick it up. If people struggle to get their luggage in an overhead bin, I jump up and help them.... If someone looks upset, I pray for him or her and ask God for guidance for whether I should speak to that person. These are now my primary

WHAT ARE SOME POSITIVE ASPECTS OF THESE GAMES?

Humor and laughter are helpful remedies for our souls, even a type of salve for our health. "Humor is infectious. The sound of roaring laughter is far more contagious than any cough, sniffle, or sneeze. When laughter is shared, it binds people together and increases happiness and intimacy. In addition to the domino effect of joy and amusement, laughter also triggers healthy physical changes in the body. Humor and laughter strengthen [our] immune system[s], boost [our] energy, diminish pain, and protect [us] from the damaging effects of stress. Best of all, this priceless medicine is fun, free, and easy to use."[5]

When we can laugh at our own inconsistencies and failures, we also recognize with humility our own inadequacies. It's okay to be human and make mistakes. It is even funny (maybe later), if the mistakes don't seriously hurt someone else. I think a loving way to enjoy humor is to tell stories that illustrate my own faults or the irony of certain situations.

I admit that I also still point out other people's inconsistencies in some humorous way—I like to think that I only do so directly to them and only pick areas where they will more likely laugh than cry over the comment. This is an area that God is still helping me work on. I also admit that saying witty comments is part of my attempts to be accepted, to be voted on the lifeboat.

I have spent a lot of time in this chapter discouraging our tendency to judge others as worse than we are. I am not trying to discourage you from making judgments. To choose is to judge. We have to judge to make daily decisions and to function as a society. We try to base our judgments and decisions on our personal value system and on our society's value system (like our laws).

As Christians, we try to base our judgments and decisions on the absolute truths we find in what the Bible says. One of our pastors has pointed out that the problem occurs when we raise our interpretation or application of the Bible's truth to the level of the authority of the Bible. We think everyone should interpret the Bible and apply the truth of the Bible in the same way we do (Be Like Me). Then we criticize and look down on those who disagree or don't follow our interpretation.

---

reasons for going to the airport, but since I'm there, I [also] catch my scheduled flight." Who knows? Maybe that was Jan Johnson helping me at the airport that morning. Johnson, *Invitation*, 85.

5. Smith et al., "Laughter is the Best Medicine," lines 1–13.

Can't we agree to dialogue about our differences without feeling superior to those who are not like us? Can't we recognize that we have all fallen short of the glory of God, so no one can boast about his choices or his works or even his interpretations of Scripture? That sounds like a place of freedom—a place I would like to live and love.

SO HOW ABOUT YOU?

1. What stories do you have like these? In other words, what Passive Be Like Me Games do you see other people playing (either ones listed in this chapter or others you can think of)? What Passive Be Like Me Games do you play?

2. In my opinion, Passive Be Like Me Gamers believe they are rarely wrong. So how about you—how often do you conclude you are wrong in your opinions or statements or actions?

    a. I am hardly ever wrong

    b. Once per week

    c. Once per day

    d. More than once per day

3. I also think that Passive Be Like Me Gamers typically judge others or try to convince others to be like them, without having that conversation directly with them. So think about your past few days. How often did you judge others without confronting them directly?

    a. Rarely

    b. Once per week

    c. Once per day

    d. More than once per day

4. What would life look like if you didn't play Passive Be Like Me Games?

7

Serve Me Games

Rather than asking you for help, I want to coerce you to get what I want, so I protect myself by manipulating you to serve me (with a Serve Me Game). Instead of playing this game, I will honestly share my desires and discuss the best action to take, while recognizing I may not get what I want.

At an August 28, 2009, memorial service for Senator Edward Kennedy, Vice-President Joe Biden recalled an early introduction to national politics, while working with more-experienced Senators Kennedy, Dick Clark, and John Culver. Biden was thanking John Culver for his opening remarks at the service, and added:

> I remember when we were talking about Angola once, and you and Teddy were working out a deal with some of our more conservative friends. We agreed on a particular course of action. . . . [Later] I was alone with . . . you and Dick and Teddy and me in Teddy's office. Being naïve as I was as a young senator, we started about how we were going to approach this issue on the floor. And Teddy said, "We gotta to do this."
> And I said, "But that's not what we said. We told these guys that we were going to do that."
> And Teddy very politely said . . . , "Well, no. We're going to do this [not what Biden remembered they promised to do]."
> And this went on for a few minutes, until finally John, in a roaring voice, said, "Biden, what the hell do you think this is—Boys State?"[1]

---

1. "Edward Kennedy Memorial Service."

Do you get what happened here? Maybe I'm naïve about this kind of thing, but here's what I heard:

- The vice president is eulogizing the death of Teddy Kennedy, one of the most powerful and compassionate senators to serve in the United States Congress. His speech is being recorded on national television. My mom would have said he was speaking in front of God and everybody.

- He opens his eulogy with a story about how he learned to not keep his word (= lie) from the man he is honoring. Deception and lying were so much a part of the political process that Culver criticized Biden (in a humorous way) for even thinking they would keep their commitment to their colleagues.

- Biden and the audience laughed at Culver's humor. In their world, this was a normal way to get others to help you get what you want—just make a promise you don't plan to keep.

I have thought about this incident a lot, much more than normal for me. I am not really into politics, and maybe this story confirms why. As I pondered Biden's "no-big-deal" admission to lying to get others to help them, I thought:

- I couldn't do that—admit I was lying in front of God and everybody, on national television. Not without at least apologizing for my deception. Or, at least not without acting like I was sorry for my deception. Or, at least not without trying to rationalize my deception. (Obviously, I need to improve on my willingness to share what is really going on in my life—maybe re-read chapter 4 about those Isolation Games I tend to play.)

- Kennedy and others were playing the ultimate Serve Me Game—lying and deception. I lie to get you to help me do what I want to do.

- Actually, why would we need to play the other Serve Me Games? Lying and deception seem so straightforward. That game of lying is not nearly as hard to play. It's so easy and obvious that I am not even sure it should be called a game.

Then the answer came to me. Why do we need to play the other Serve Me Games? Trust. When I play my Serve Me Games, I still want you to trust me. In this situation, I don't see how the Kennedy's colleagues could ever trust him again, after they were double-crossed on the Senate floor. When it is so blatant, so obvious, so normal to lie, how does anyone trust someone else at all?

Okay. Now I feel better (or worse). We have a reason to review the Serve Me Games. They do serve a purpose, in a twisted sort of way, allowing me to disguise my desire for you to serve me. I need you to help me get what I want, but I don't want to risk asking you to help me, because you might say "No." Instead, I use a Serve Me Game to manipulate you to get what I want, without taking the chance that you might refuse to help me. And if I deceive you with my game, you still trust me.

While there may be many Serve Me Games, I have identified two different examples for our review:

- Guilt Game
- One-Sided Win-Win Game

PLAYING THE GUILT GAME

Mothers are known for their ability to play the Guilt Game. You know, this is the game where mom tries to get you to do something for her, by making you feel guilty if you don't do it. Some typical examples are:

- Have you been to church lately? (You are letting her down if you don't go, with an implied message that you are letting God down, too.)
- We haven't seen you and your family since March. When are you planning to come see us again? (You should already feel guilty for taking so long to visit her, and the guilt will compound if you don't come soon.)
- The neighbors were commenting on how shoddy my yard looks. You know, Doris's son mows her lawn for her. (Obviously, if you cared about your mom as much as Doris's son cares about his mom, you would have already mowed your mom's lawn. You better get over there and mow it soon to at least stop these guilt-producing comments.)

Mothers (and fathers) aren't the only ones who use guilt to motivate others to serve them. It seems to be especially common in church life. Recently, one church's pastor gave a sermon in the morning that pointed out that Christ had freed us from guilt. That same afternoon another pastor in the same church was trying to motivate his members to join a prayer circle by saying he was monitoring the list of members who signed up for the prayer circle. It was hard to not feel guilty for not signing up for the prayer circle.

Another pastor had been invited to give the invocation at the opening of a new chain store in his home town. He was planning to include in his prayer to God some statements intended for the chain-store managers—statements about paying a fair wage and supporting fair trade. I wonder if the chain-store managers got the message of guilt, in the midst of this prayer of thanksgiving.

Beth points out that our feelings of guilt can come from our own "stuff." For example, the question from mom, "Have you been to church lately?" probably wouldn't make you feel guilty if mom asks, "Have you been to a good restaurant lately?" You assume mom attaches some value judgment to attending church, but she is not trying to get you to eat out at restaurants. In each of these mom examples, you are probably playing the ESP Game with mom's comments, assuming she is trying to "guilt" you into going to church, coming to see her, or mow her lawn. Don't get me wrong—you may be playing the ESP Game accurately, but you really don't know without asking her.

The Guilt Game can also be played in a more subtle manner. You can throw in the phrase, "We need to _____" and it sounds less intimidating—almost passive-aggressive. Oops! I meant almost passive. For example, when I tell Beth, "We need to stop spending so much on the house," I really mean, "I want you to stop spending so much on the house."

Shelley, a friend of ours, puts this passive version of the Guilt Game into action instead of words. She doesn't verbalize the "We need to _____." She just starts doing the "We need to _____" job. Let's say Shelley wants her husband, Pierre, to organize his tool bench. After fair warning that Pierre's tool bench needs to be organized, she just starts organizing his tools herself one Saturday morning when Pierre is around the house. Shelley knows that Pierre cannot stand for her to be messing with his tools, so sure enough, he takes over the project and sends Shelley off to some other chore. Pierre is now organizing his tools, so Shelley has succeeded with this action version of the Guilt Game.

THE SCIENCE OF GUILT

It took me years of discussions with Beth to figure out this game, since Beth played the game so well. This combination of science and gamesmanship is very sophisticated, so most people don't even notice they are playing the game until we explain it to them. Think of it as a scientific form of nagging, which I call the Science of Guilt. It's scientific, because Beth is relying on the "proven" principle of cause and effect to make her guilt-inducing point.

It is a way for Beth (or anyone for that matter) to send a guilt-producing reminder to me to change something in my life, something that she has brought up before. Actually, I would be changing for Beth. Of course, she doesn't say that the change would benefit her at all—she is just thinking about my welfare, since this event obviously shows that I should change.

The process goes something like this:

- Beth has some concern about the way I act. Let's say that she wants to convince me to clean up my mess in the closet.

- Something bad happens to me. It may or may not be related to my unorganized mess in the closet. Let's say I misplace my car keys and can't find them. This is the "effect" Beth has been looking for.

- Beth ties the unfortunate event (the loss of my keys = the effect) to the area of my life that she thinks I should change (the messy closet = the cause). It doesn't matter if they are really connected as cause and effect. In this example, she "innocently" makes an observation, "You know, you probably could find your car keys if you cleaned up the mess in the closet." It even sounds scientific—we have the cause and the effect wrapped up in clear guilt-inducing logic. Obviously, it is my best interest to clean up my closet (and find my keys), not just her personal preference.

- She doesn't say what she really thinks and feels, such as, "Your messy closet is unnerving to me." She has subtly made her point (again) that my closet is messy and needs to be cleaned up.

PLAYING THE ONE-SIDED WIN-WIN GAME

I identified my ability to use a Win-Win strategy early in my career. It is actually a helpful strategy in the business world. When negotiating an agreement in that world, I found that compromise is essential. If we both feel like we win something important as part of the compromise, we have achieved a win-win result. We can both feel good about the agreement.

So far, the Win-Win strategy seems pretty straightforward—it sounds more like an effective way to negotiate an agreement, not a manipulative game. In the One-Sided Win-Win Game, I take this a step further. I selectively disclose enough information (tell half-truths) for you to agree to apparently get your way, while holding back information that might discourage you from agreeing with my solution. I win and you think you win. Of course, you could be playing the same game, so the end result is we are both surprised by the final outcome. I thought I won, but I didn't. You thought you won, but you didn't. Now, neither one of us can trust the other person, because we each discovered that the other person was selectively disclosing critical information. No wonder we are all so skeptical of each other and continue to play ESP Games!

We can play this same game in our personal relationships. For example, Beth and I have just gotten a $2,000 income-tax refund and we are trying to decide what to do with the extra money. By nature, we are both givers, so we allocate $300 to help a friend with some unexpected expenses. At this point, we typically disagree on what to do with the remaining $1,700. I am a saver who thinks spending money on stuff for me is selfish, and Beth is a spender who thinks hoarding money (saving) is miserly. You can tell this gets personal for each of us. So we compromise to resolve this dispute, hopefully in a loving manner:

- We agree to split the $1,700 in half—$850 goes into our 401(k) plan for retirement (my preference) and $850 goes to replace an older chair in our living room (Beth's preference). So far, so good. No gaming here, at least not anything obvious.
- I actually know about some other funds coming our way. The $2,000 income-tax refund was just the federal income-tax refund. We also got a $100 state income-tax refund, which I didn't disclose. In my accounting terms, the $100 amount was immaterial—too small to throw into this discussion. That's how I rationalize hiding this fact from Beth. So I actually get to save $950 into the 401(k) plan.

- Beth knows the chair she wants actually will cost $1,000 by the time sales tax and delivery charges are included. She doesn't disclose this fact in our discussions. Later, the chair is delivered with the invoice and she acts surprised, "Gee, I didn't think about the taxes and delivery. The chair really costs $1,000 with all these added fees, not $850. It really looks good here, doesn't it? Do you just want me to send it back?" You can hear the innocent, pleading tone in her voice.

We just manipulated each other in the One-Sided Win-Win Game, so we could each get a little more of what we wanted, without taking the risk of asking. Serve me. Just don't know that you are serving me. I feel slimy just writing out the example.

WHERE DO WE FEEL THREATENED? HOW DO WE TRY TO PROTECT OURSELVES WITH THESE GAMES?

It seems to me that I play most of the Serve Me Games for one of three reasons:

- I want you to do something for me. I am afraid that if I just tell you what I want that you will say "No." Thus, I need to play one of these games to manipulate you to give me what I want.

- I want you to do something for me. I am afraid that if I just tell you what I want that you will judge me as self-centered for being so selfish, thinking that it is all about me. Then you will reject me. I am trying to protect some semblance of a relationship (your acceptance of me) while I still get what I want with one of these games.

- Sometimes I'm also afraid that I won't accomplish my To-Do List, which puts me at risk in somebody's lifeboat. If I don't get this task done, somebody will be disappointed in me—maybe just me, but of all people, I don't want to disappoint me. Unfortunately, in these cases I am in "task mode," so I am not even pretending that these other people are worth a relationship—they are solely there as a resource to serve me. They might as well be robots. Loving them or caring about them is not even on my radar.

WHAT ARE THE UNINTENDED MESSAGES WE ARE SENDING?

In my opinion, I think I have fooled you with my games. I think you don't see me manipulating you to serve me. I may actually fool you for a while. While I am fooling you, I just look inconsistent—you are not sure what feels odd about my actions, but something is not quite right with the way I act.

Eventually you figure it out. Once you grasp how I am playing these Serve Me Games, I lose your trust—the trust I hoped to salvage by playing these games. You feel used. I send you the message that I really don't care about you—you are just a resource to serve me. You resent the whole relationship.

WHAT ARE SOME LOVING SOLUTIONS TO REPLACE THESE GAMES?

I am afraid I won't get what I want, so I play the Serve Me Games. What is the worst thing that can happen if I don't get what I want? Mmmmm, that's an interesting question. I would be disappointed, maybe frustrated, and maybe angry. Who knows? I might actually be better off if I don't get what I want. So how do I know?

Maybe if I trusted you and felt accepted by you, no matter what I say, I could share with you what I was thinking I wanted. You could share the same with me. We could actually brainstorm whether what we each wanted was out of love or not. You know, we could even pray together to ask God to give us guidance. Am I just being selfish or is this appropriate self-care? Am I really trying to help these other people, or am I just trying to look good in front of my other friends? Then I wouldn't have to play these games to get you to serve me. You would actually be choosing to serve me out of love, not out of manipulation. I would actually have some independent feedback that what I was wanting was either appropriate or not. This sounds like the type of relationships I would like to have. This sounds so simple, yet so hard to carry out.

To overcome my "task mode" tendencies, I first have to let go of the need to accomplish the entire To-Do List. It has to drop in priority, compared to loving the people I encounter while working on my To-Do List. If God puts someone in my path with a specific need I can meet, I have to recognize that is potentially more important than the task I am working on. I have to stop thinking of these people as robots whose only purpose is to serve me. This sounds trickier to figure out—there is no formula. I need to trust God to open my eyes to their needs and to take care of items on my To-Do List that just don't get done on time.

WHAT ARE SOME POSITIVE ASPECTS OF THESE GAMES?

It is hard to find a positive aspect to manipulating other people, and that is the primary goal of the Serve Me Games. I do see some positives in using the Win-Win strategy, as long as it is done openly and honestly. I also see some positives to being committed to accomplishing tasks on my To-Do List. Some of those items on the list are tasks I am doing out of love and commitment to serving other people. Keeping my commitments to these people seems appropriate, as long as I am not over-committing myself and as long as I also care about the people I encounter while working on my To-Do List.

SO HOW ABOUT YOU?

1. What stories do you have like these? In other words, what Serve Me Games do you see other people playing (either ones listed in this chapter or others you can think of)? What Serve Me Games do you play?
2. Over the last few days how often have you tried to manipulate others to do what you want them to do?
    a. I didn't try to manipulate them to serve me during the last few days
    b. Once during the last few days
    c. Once per day
    d. More than one time per day
3. What would life look like if you didn't play Serve Me Games?

8

Looking Good Games

I want to earn your respect, so I protect my self-worth by manipulating situations to make myself look good (with a Looking Good Game). Instead of playing this game, I will openly share the truth about myself, trusting that God loves me like I am (and you might, too).

Have you ever starting playing a new sport? You learn how to play the new game, and just as importantly, you also learn the look. You definitely want to match the special look to show that you belong. You portray an air of confidence with the look. You know what you are doing, because you look like you know what you are doing. You see it all the time. Bicyclists cruise the roads in those tight pants and loud shirts. Basketball players jump higher with their favorite brand of basketball shoes. Hikers enjoy the great outdoors in their wicking clothing and comfortable, yet durable hiking boots.

Inevitably, the sport newbie recognizes that others are going to find out that she really is just learning this sport. So what does she say to her companions, as she swings around, pretending to survey her stunning attire in an invisible mirror? "You know, I can look good, even if I can't be good."

We don't only use that logic with our favorite sport. We sometimes apply the same logic to life. One of our family counselors recognized that fact and made it so clear with this succinct question, "Would you rather just look good or would you rather be good?"

What a penetrating question! How would you answer it? I confess there are times when I am content with just looking good. I don't really have to be good as long as I look good. I don't think I'm alone. That is why I have reserved this last chapter for the Looking Good Games. Look at two of the ways we try to look good:

- False Humility Game
- Martyr Game

By the way, some of the other games have included a "looking good" aspect. For example:

- The Isolation Gamer thinks through what he says (before he says it) to be sure his statements sound wise and not foolish.
- The Avoiding Responsibility Gamer doesn't want to get caught or at least blamed for her decisions.
- The Passive Be Like Me Gamer wants you to be like her without looking like she wants to control your life.
- The Serve Me Gamer wants you to serve him while he appears trustworthy.

It seems to me that in each of these games, the person playing the game has another, more pressing motive—withdrawing in safety, avoiding consequences, convincing others he is right, and coercing others to help him get what he wants. In the Looking Good Games, the gamer's primary motive is to be respected by looking good. So let's look at some ways we settle for just looking good.

> **LOOKING GOOD WHEN EMBARRASSED**
>
> When we go to the beach, I hope we have waves big enough to body surf, but not too big to bring out the red warning flags. In case you didn't know, there are several risks to body surfing. I won't get into the less common jelly fish, shark, or undertow risks. The most common risk is not catching the wave at the right point. In that case, the wave can just pound me into the sand or it can violently flip me over and over. Fortunately, I usually catch the wave close enough to the right point and have an exciting ride to the shore, or I just miss it altogether and have to wait for the next promising wave.
>
> Beth and I were recently at the beach for the week. It was a sunny day, and Goldilocks would have liked the waves—they were not too big, they were not too little, they were just right. So I was catching

some good waves and enjoying myself, until I caught a big wave at the wrong point. The wave flipped me over and around, and the force yanked my swimsuit down toward my feet. Fortunately, I felt my swimsuit coming off and I grabbed it at my ankles. If someone could have seen me in the wave, I would have looked so funny. I was being tossed around inside the wave, holding my swimsuit onto my ankles with one hand and the rest of my body flailing around within the wave.

In a few seconds it was over. I found myself lying face down in the shallow water at the shore, still holding my swimsuit with one hand at my ankles. Obviously, I didn't want to risk standing up to pull up my swimsuit. So I remained flat on my stomach in the shallow water. I reached down with my other hand to grab the opposite side of the swimsuit and nonchalantly started pulling it up to my waist. While I was trying to pull it up, the remnants of another wave washed over me and made me lose my grip on my swimsuit—fortunately just one hand let go. Even so, I was still glad to be bopped by this latest wave, because that gave me deeper water to finish pulling up my swimsuit. Finally, I got the swimsuit up to my waist and quickly stood up to avoid getting hit by the leftover parts of the next wave.

So what was the first thing I did when I stood up? You guessed it. I looked around to see if anyone had seen me redressing myself in the water. Or to put that differently, to see if anyone saw my private parts exposed by the wave. Or me struggling to not show my private parts, while being smacked around by more waves. Fortunately, no one had seen me (at least no one looked like they were looking my way). How embarrassing that would have been! I wanted to see if I should be more embarrassed or if I had retained some semblance of looking good.

Isn't this ironic? I didn't know anyone else at the beach. Yet I was mostly concerned about how I looked, even more concerned than with whether I was physically hurt. While my reaction was pretty normal, it illustrates a basic truth—our identities are so easily dictated by how we look to others. Sounds like a lifeboat issue to me.

PLAYING THE FALSE HUMILITY GAME

What character trait is important to you and your friends? Many of my friends value humility. We want to be humble. I think we actually then take this a step further—each of us wants to appear humble, even when we are not really humble. For example:

- I am afraid that something I am getting ready to say will offend you, but I want to say it anyway. I also want to look like I care about offending you. I think I can get away with making my statement by starting with, "I'm sorry, but . . . "

- I have an opinion about how something should be done, but I don't want to look like I am a know-it-all. I don't want to be domineering in my approach. So I start my sentence with, "In my humble opinion . . . "

- I have done something that I feel proud of—let's say I shot a 79 in a round of golf. I don't just walk up to a fellow golfer and say I shot a 79. That would not appear humble. Instead, I ask my friend, "Have you played any golf lately?" I hope he asks me the same question, and then I can tell him about my unbelievable round, shooting a 79. Even then, I don't give too many details, unless he asks, because I still don't want to appear that proud. It is a game of golf, after all.

I am playing the False Humility Game. I am not really humble at all, but I want to appear humble.

There are many related games—just substitute the character trait that is important in the situation. With my clients and my manager, it is important to work hard and be responsive. If I can't be responsive, at least I want to look responsive. When I do that, I am playing a related game—the related False Responsiveness Game. For example, I am on a phone call with my manager. She asks about the status of some request she made last week. "Dang it all," I think, "I forgot all about that request." I don't say what I am thinking, because that would not look responsive. "I haven't got that information yet," I say, "but it's at the top of my To-Do List." That's not far from the truth—it sure rose to the top of my To-Do List as soon as she asked me again for this information. I wasn't responsive, but I now appear as responsive as I can under the circumstances because I told her that it has top priority. It certainly has top priority now. I think I look better (more responsive) to my boss than I would have, if I had just said that I forgot about her request.

One final example, flipping from the dedicated-employee role to the dedicated-husband role—actually the False Dedicated Husband. Remember the Blame Game scenario in chapter 3? It started with Beth confronting me with being late, "Why are you just now getting home? I told you this morning that we have a dinner with the Smiths tonight at 6:30 in Greensboro."

You know, this conflict really didn't start when I got home. It started two hours earlier, as I stopped to assess where I was on my project at work. I made a decision at that point that kept me from getting home on time. I acted like I just forgot about the time and our dinner. I actually looked at the clock around 4:30 and thought to myself, "I would like to finish this project before I go home. We do have dinner tonight with the Smiths, but I think I have time to get it done. Maybe I should call Beth and see what she thinks. Nah—I already know what she thinks. She'll want me to come on home and figure out the project some other time. This part of the project is really fun. Let's see if I can't get this finished in the next hour."

So two hours later (not the one hour I expected) I arrived home and Beth confronted me with being late. As a true False Dedicated Husband, I wanted to look as good as possible to Beth. So I didn't disclose my 4:30 discussion with myself. That confession could send Beth the message that I really preferred work over her, and I don't want to look like that to Beth. So I tried to change from the dedicated employee who enjoys solving client problems to the dedicated, loving husband who just made a human error and misunderstood our plans for the evening. It became another not-so-white lie to look good—did I get away with this one?

I think we all play this Looking Good Game—trying to look better than we really are. The name changes based on the character trait where we want to look good. So the name of this game probably should be the False _____ Game (you fill in the blank with your desired character trait, at least the desired character trait you want to display right now). All for the purpose of looking better than we really are.

PLAYING THE MARTYR GAME

Martyr = a person who sacrifices something of great value and especially life itself for the sake of principle or religion.[1]

Do you ever think of yourself as a martyr? Religious martyrs were persecuted and actually sacrificed their lives to stay true to their religious convictions. Many still do. We have taken this term and applied it to much less serious types of sacrifice (kind of like we have done with the term "passive-aggressive"). We modified the meaning so that I can present myself as a martyr and get the same "respect" that we give to real martyrs.

I see and feel (and maybe resent) all I have given up for you and I want credit, so I play the Martyr Game. I want to look good while I "lovingly" sacrifice my wants and needs for you, and I want you to appreciate it. If I didn't get what I really wanted, at least give me my due—recognition and praise for sacrificing myself. For example:

- Mom to her rebellious teenager, "After all I have done for you, you treat me like this! I birthed you in pain, gave up my career for you, sent you to the best schools, and you don't respect me at all. You think the world revolves around you!"

- Employee to his manager, "Well, I am supposed to be on vacation that day. If you really need for me to call in to this meeting, I will find the time that day. Just remember this at review time."

- Overworked volunteer talking to her friend, "It sounds like you are having a rough time. I would like to get together sometime this week. Let's see, I work with the internationals on Monday night, I lead a women's group on Tuesday night, and of course, choir is Wednesday night. I think I am open this Thursday. You know, I just don't think I ever have time for myself."

You get the picture. I want to look good by showing you how much I am sacrificing for you or others. Hopefully you will respect me even more, once you recognize (through my Martyr Game) how much I have given up for you or for a common cause. If I'm successful, I will be "looking good in the neighborhood."

---

1 Merriam-Webster Dictionary, s.v. "martyr," accessed May 17, 2011. Online: http://www.merriam-webster.com/dictionary/martyr.

WHERE DO WE FEEL THREATENED? HOW DO WE TRY TO PROTECT OURSELVES WITH THESE GAMES?

Boy! This is a no-brainer! Why am I trying to protect myself? What am I afraid of when I am trying to look good? I must feel threatened by the possibility of looking bad.

Okay. Maybe we can go a little deeper. What is so bad about looking bad? Well, I may have to pay some consequences for my "bad" actions. I don't want to get caught looking bad, if it means I will get a ticket or get reprimanded by my boss or be judged by my friends. I don't want to admit I am as "bad" as I really am.

Or, put another way, what is so good about looking good? I think I will be more respected and accepted and loved if I look good. Taking this one more step, I don't think you will respect or accept or love me, unless I look good.

Bingo! This could be it. I believe I have to earn your respect and your love. I know I am not always good enough to earn your love, so I need to look better than I really am. It's another lifeboat feeling. If I look good enough, you won't vote me out of the lifeboat.

WHAT ARE THE UNINTENDED MESSAGES WE ARE SENDING?

It seems to me that we are sending several unintended messages when we play Looking Good Games:

- What if the other person actually believes my charade and thinks I am as good as I look? The intended message is I am worthy of respect. The unintended message is the only way I think I will be respected is if I am good. So, the other person may flip that message on themselves. For example, he may say to himself, "Obviously, Joe thinks working hard is important. I'm not that committed to working hard. Joe probably doesn't respect my choice to not work as hard. Joe probably doesn't even respect me."

- What if the other person sees through my charade and sees that I am not as good as I try to appear? The unintended message is I am a hypocrite. I am a chameleon playing the False _____ Game. I don't just abandon my values when convenient to do so. When

I play a Looking Good Game, I still act like I have stayed true to my values.

- Whether the other person buys into my Looking Good message or not, I probably send out a message of arrogance and pride. I want you to know how good I am, so I still look boastful and full of myself.

> **Looking Good as an Ambassador for Christ**
>
> Various passages in the New Testament encourage Christians to be loving and blameless in their culture, at least partly to attract others to faith in Christ. We Christians consider ourselves ambassadors for Christ (2 Cor 5:20), and we certainly don't want to let Christ down. The formula goes something like this:
>
>
>
> Joe lives a righteous and loving life
>
>
>
> Non-believer admires Joe and wants to be like Joe
>
>
>
> Non-believer might give his heart to Christ
> (since Joe is more loving, now that he is a Christian)
>
>
>
> So what happens when I don't act out of love— when I play one of these relationship games? Or even worse, a family member or I commit one of the more obvious sexual or illegal sins—then what happens? I think I am tempted to look good, since I can't be good. I have let Christ down on my end of the formula. So I deal with my shame over the issue by denying it or hiding it, hoping that the non-believer doesn't notice that I (or my family) didn't live up to our Christian values.
>
> I think we Christians send these same unintended messages when we don't admit our "stuff" to each other and even to non-believers. They see us as arrogant or hypocritical or both. What if we stop playing the Looking Good Games and just confess our challenges and failures to one another (James 5:16)? What if we keep everything we do and say out in the open, . . . [refusing] to wear masks and [refusing to] play games (2 Cor 4:2 MSG)? Maybe God's unconditional love and grace will shine through, in spite of us. Maybe when we aren't loving, the formula might look like this:

> Joe humbly apologizes for not loving others like Christ
> ⇒
> Joe shares that Christ loves and accepts him anyway
> ⇒
> Non-believer admires Christ and wants to be like Christ
> ⇒
> Non-believer might give his heart to Christ
>
> What a relief! I no longer have to look good to be an ambassador for Christ. I can admit my "stuff" without letting Christ down. Actually, I am an ambassador for Christ when I am honest about my life—our (God's and my) victories and my struggles.
>
> Don't get me wrong—God is certainly most glorified when I am open to his spirit and love him and others as Christ did. The Lord doesn't need me to look good. He obviously prefers that I just be good *and* authentic.

WHAT ARE SOME LOVING SOLUTIONS TO REPLACE THESE GAMES?

What if I don't care whether I look good or not? What if the call of the mythical lifeboat, the call to justify myself to others, has no power over me? Think about that one for a minute. Feel that idea for a minute. What would life be like? That solution sure sounds like a logical, loving solution.

When I ponder this question, my first feeling is one of freedom, similar to the freedom I felt when I thought about not playing some of the other relationship games. I think it is a freedom to be real about what I really believe and what I really do. I feel free from having to look good. It's not that I don't want to be loved and accepted. It's just that I am willing to sacrifice that opportunity for your love and respect if you are only going to love and respect me when you think I am good. I am willing to look to God alone for that unconditional love, if I have to. God's love is enough, and I know it is unconditional.

My second feeling is one of fear. What did I just say? This sounds like a lonely, uncertain place—not earning the respect of others, having to trust them to love me unconditionally. I know how those other people think. They think like I do—I can fall into judging others for their failures and requiring them to earn my respect. How do I expect them to love me unconditionally, when I sometimes don't love them unconditionally?

My last feeling is one of acceptance and trust. I realize that looking good isn't working. I am sending all kinds of unintended messages. If I am real about my stuff (both my attempts at love and my failures), you might even respect me more. At least you would feel comfortable trusting me—if I didn't hide my stuff, if I didn't try to look good. I would feel better about myself. And if it doesn't work out, if you have lost respect for me and no longer care about me, I am willing to trust that God has a different journey for me than I wanted. Hopefully, I will return your conditional love/judgment with unconditional love. Hopefully, someone else will accept me unconditionally. Hopefully, God will flood me with his overwhelming love.

WHAT ARE SOME POSITIVE ASPECTS OF THESE GAMES?

It is difficult to find a positive aspect to trying to look good. Obviously, if I am successful at looking good, I will probably be more successful in meeting my worldly goals. I think it is hard to continue to look good for a long period of time, without actually being good. So I may have some short-term rewards for looking good.

At times, I am motivated to be more responsible and more loving because I want to look good. In this case, looking good is actually encouraging me to be good. That motive is not the most honorable reason to treat others well, but I may develop loving habits that end up improving my motives in the future. God seems to work that way sometimes, changing my attitude as I decide to act out of love.

SO HOW ABOUT YOU?

1. What stories do you have like these? In other words, what Looking Good Games do you see other people playing (either ones listed in this chapter or others you can think of)? What Looking Good Games do you play?
2. Over the past few days, how often did you intentionally make a decision that you believed would make you look good to others?
    a. Didn't make any decisions to make myself look good
    b. Once during the last few days
    c. Once per day
    d. More than once per day
3. What would life look like if you didn't play Looking Good Games?

Section Two

The Game Changer:
Letting Go of the Outcome

9

Imagining a Life Without Our Games

WHEW! WE MADE IT through all these relationship games. And just think—you may have thought of other games that I haven't even covered.

So how are you feeling now? I am a little down—thinking about all the games I play that cripple my relationships. It's been fun to name the games, but trying to figure out why I play the games can be depressing and overwhelming. That's why I like to think through the loving solutions which replace these games. They give me a vision, maybe a challenging one, but still a vision of living out of love instead of self-protection. What will life be like if we don't play these games? Take a moment to imagine that type of world—it feels comforting to me.

WHAT ARE THE LOVING SOLUTIONS FOR OUR GAMES?

Here's a chart of our games, along with the possible loving solutions to the games. (One couple liked this chart so much that they put a copy of it on the door of their refrigerator, as a reminder to each other to replace their games with more authentic ways to live. No assignment that you do the same thing—it's just a thought to post it on your fridge or even your cubicle at work.) Let me give you some guidance on reading this chart, while visualizing what an authentic life of love looks like. You repeat the heading as you read each row. For example, reading the first row sounds like this:

> Instead of speculating about your motives and intentions (with an ESP Game), I will let go of my desire to avoid the possible pain of you taking advantage of me, and in love I will take the time to listen to you, ask you questions, and seek to understand you.

Instead of . . .	I will let go of my desire to . . .	and in love I will . . .
speculating about your motives and intentions (with an ESP Game),	avoid the possible pain of you taking advantage of me	take the time to listen to you, ask you questions, and seek to understand you.
refusing to improve or change myself (with a Don't Change Me Game),	avoid the possible pain of changing	recognize change is inevitable and ask God what to change and how to change.
blaming others for my situation (with an Avoiding Responsibility Game),	avoid my responsibility and the consequences of my actions	accept my role in this situation, state my fears, and apologize if appropriate.
keeping my thoughts and feelings to myself (with an Isolation Game),	play it safe and avoid embarrassing myself	connect with you by sharing my feelings, my stories, my hopes, and my disappointments.
pushing you to live your life like I do (with a Be Perfect Like Me Game),	convince you that I am right and influence (control) your actions	humbly recognize I don't know it all and just ask you to consider my idea.
judging and criticizing you behind your back (with a Passive Be Like Me Game),	prove I am better than you	recognize I don't know it all and listen and empathize with you, and if needed confront you with humility.
manipulating you to serve me (with a Serve Me Game),	trick you to get what I want	honestly share my desires, and discuss the best action to take while recognizing I may not get what I want.
working to make myself look good (with a Looking Good Game),	earn your respect	openly share myself, trusting that God loves me like I am (and you might, too).

Wow! Can I live like that? Can I really let go of my need to protect myself in all these games and instead let it all go in loving others? How about you—can you live like this? I am looking forward to section 2, where we can review a game changer to help us actually live out these loving solutions. Maybe we can make this vision a reality in our lives. I really do want to live more honestly with my friends, family, neighbors, and co-workers, even if it means letting go of the need to protect myself.

HOW DO WE KNOW WHAT GAMES WE ARE PLAYING?

You may have trouble figuring out which game you are playing at the moment. It helps to be aware of your thoughts and feelings, even if you have to evaluate the event after-the-fact. If you hurt someone, that just gives you the opportunity to apologize, which frequently improves the relationship. See if you can identify what motive is pushing you to manipulate others, perhaps what is making you feel threatened or fearful. How are you trying to protect yourself?

These self-protective motives are the threats that subconsciously undermine our loving intentions, leading us to play games in our relationships. In the above chart, the threats you may feel are shown in the middle column. For example, when I feel skeptical about your intentions and concerned that you will take advantage of me, I am likely to play an ESP Game. Check out the middle column to see where you may be trying to protect your self-interest. Which self-protective motive best describes your situation? That is a good indicator of the type of game you may be playing.

Now as you review the chapter-by-chapter summary of the games we have explored in section 1, take a close look at the possible self-protective motives (in italics) for playing each game:

- ESP Games—*how we are concerned that another person will take advantage of us*, so we speculate about that person's motives or feelings, and then we act on our speculations. We worked on asking what the other person is thinking or feeling—maybe by using reflective listening or even just stating to that person what we are afraid he is thinking. We also discussed the more loving option of actually caring enough to get to know him and help him instead of speculating.

- Don't Change Me Games—*how we feel threatened by losing control over our lives, so we exert the ultimate control and refuse to try to change.* "It's my life and this is just the way I am," we say to ourselves. It's a way to avoid responsibility for future decisions or actions (even inaction). We miss seeing that change is inevitable, nothing is secure. We really can't change to become the composite person that everyone else wants us to be. So we discussed embracing change by asking God what to change in our lives.

- Avoiding Responsibility Games—*how we try to avoid the consequences of our decisions and actions* by blaming others and by going on the offensive. We even discussed how we act like we apologize, when we don't really mean to apologize at all. We identified the more loving option of just taking responsibility and apologizing for our actions and decisions, while stating our fears to the other person (where we are afraid of the possible consequences of accepting the blame).

- Isolation Games—*how some of us (especially introverts) play it safe with various Isolation Games, when we avoid disclosing our opinions and feelings to others.* Then we reviewed a couple of ways to open up—sharing three events from each day (including our feelings about those events) and sharing our stories with each other (stories from our past and our ideas about the future).

- Be Perfect Like Me Games—*how we want to convince others that we are right and influence (control) their decisions*, so we push them to act and (hopefully) think the same way we do. To avoid playing these games, we were encouraged to trade our arrogance for humility—recognize we really aren't as smart as we think we are. Also watch out for when we are feeling smug, or superior, or frustrated, or attacked—in all those cases, we may be trying to force others to be like us. Instead of insisting others change, we use the power of the request and just ask.

- Passive Be Like Me Games—*how some of us want to prove we are better than others, without confronting the issue directly.* We reviewed some of the Be Like Me "humility" strategies to live more lovingly, since they also apply to the Passive Be Like Me Gamer. We who play the Passive Be Like Me Games can also overcome the need to protect ourselves by learning to deal with our fear of conflict—replacing the threat of conflict with a desire to confront others with love and humility. Finally, we can become more empathetic (and less judging) by listening to others' experiences, and realizing that we could be like them or that we are actually like them.

- Serve Me Games—*how we are concerned we will not get what we want and we need others' help to satisfy our desires,* so we either manipulate others to serve us or just treat them as a means get what we want. We identified a loving option to recognize that everything we want may not be best for us. If we agree with that idea, we can be open with others about what we want and discuss with them the pros and cons of our plans. We can trust that if we don't get something accomplished or something we wanted, that God will work it out anyway.

- Looking Good Games—*how we are concerned others will not respect us unless we look good.* We discussed the loving solution to not worry about how we look to other people—to not try to earn their respect by looking good. Instead, trust God that he and even some other people will love and respect us, no matter how we look.

WHAT DOES AN AUTHENTIC LIFESTYLE LOOK LIKE?

As we imagine a world where we don't play these relationship games, let's consider what the end result might look like. We need a vision of authentic living, so we can plan how to get there and so we can recognize it when we succeed in living this way. So, in a perfect world what are the key elements of a loving and honest relationship—a relationship built on trust and mutual respect? What does this look like, when love permeates our relationships? You may have others, but I came up with these essential characteristics:

- First, we will know ourselves. We will uncover the games we play and the ingrained fears that feed these games. But that is not all—we will also recognize our thoughts and our motives, our strengths and our weaknesses, our dreams and our passions. I call this "self-awareness."

- Second, we will not keep our self-awareness to ourselves. We will be willing to share ourselves with others, both the "good" and the "bad" aspects of our character and our lives. I call this "transparency."

- Third, we will realize this is a two-way relationship. We will care about others and seek to understand them, even to the point of feeling the way they feel. I call this "empathy."

To be free to live this way—in an atmosphere of love and trust and mutual respect—our entire perspective about life needs to change. We will let go of our fears and stop trying to control the outcome. This is the game changer that transforms our attitudes. Once we let go of the outcome, we will become free to become authentic lovers:

- We will be patient and kind.
- We will not be jealous of others' success or boastful of our own.
- We will not be puffed up with pride.
- We will live honorably and properly, not rudely or disgracefully.
- We will not be selfish or demand our own way—in essence, we will not be self-centered.
- We will not be irritable, and we will keep no record of wrongs.
- We will rejoice with the truth.
- Rather than rejoicing in the misfortune of others, we will protect and trust them.
- We will remain hopeful and persevere through all our challenges.[1]

Wow! What a vision! To convert this vision into a lifestyle of authentic living, let's examine this game changer—letting go of the outcome, a complete change in our attitude. I'm ready. Let's rise up and be transformed!

> **The Visual Vision**
>
> Here's another memory hook—a visual reminder of this vision of authentic living. You may want to copy this picture and put it on your refrigerator or in your cubicle, next to the chart of games and loving solutions. Instead of just trying to stop playing my games, I want to concentrate on fulfilling this vision of authentic living and loving—self-aware, transparent, empathetic, and letting go of the outcome. That's why I think this picture deserves equal space on your refrigerator. When I concentrate on these four traits of authentic living, my relationship games lose their power over my life!

---

1. Morris, *1 Corinthians*, 180–182.

10

Letting Go: Steps 1 and 2: Relieving the Pressure

One of our household traditions is an annual cookout to celebrate the Fourth of July. We invite local friends and family and enjoy food, games, and some fireworks. Almost every year we have a ping-pong (table tennis) tournament. Our sons and the rest of our friends and family seem to really get into this ping-pong challenge. At least I tell myself that they get pumped up for the tournament.

Have you ever played doubles in ping-pong? It's hilarious! Each team has two players (must be where the doubles name came from—thank you, Captain Obvious). The teammates have to take turns hitting the ping-pong ball, so each one has to hit the ball and then get out of the way so his teammate is prepared to return the next volley from the other side of the table. Inevitably, the team members run into each other or don't get out of the way in time or they just mess up. It's funny to watch. The seriously competitive ones get frustrated, but they try to hide their frustration since everyone else is watching and laughing. Remember—it's just a game!

To add to the challenge for the competitive ones, we draw names from a hat. We randomly pair up one male with one female on each team. Of course, the whining starts immediately, if two good players are randomly selected on the same team. If one of our competitive players gets "stuck" with a less skillful male teammate, she has to try to be nice and bite her tongue about her lousy luck in the random drawing for her teammate. (Yes, you read this correctly. Many of our competitive ones are female.) Then the tournament begins.

At a recent tournament, our oldest son, Steve, was paired up with Lola, who was new to the game of doubles ping-pong. Steve falls in the category of being competitive, without wanting to show that he is competitive (kind of like his Dad). Lola was just happy to hit the ball over the net when it was her turn. You could tell she felt badly about causing their team to lose points.

And that is what they were doing—losing points. They were behind in their first game, apparently destined to lose to the other team. Steve called a strategic time out and pulled Lola over to the side to discuss their next play. He held his ping-pong paddle over his mouth so the other team couldn't see the secret plan he was setting up. Lola leaned her head closer to Steve's paddle, ready to listen and apply his covert line of attack. She hoped this would be it—an effective strategy to pull out victory from the jaws of defeat. Steve tilted his head closer to Lola and whispered, "Play better." I think we can all agree with this assessment—what a useless piece of advice! Funny, but useless.

That's almost how I see this book to this point. In section 1, we identified the games we play. We have touched on some loving solutions to the games, but we have also seen plenty of examples where we (especially I) have failed by playing these games, even after knowing the loving solutions. Although something deep inside me yearns for intimacy and authenticity, I hold back because I am afraid. I keep playing these relationship games, even when I know better. Some of my advice to this point rests on recognizing our games and choosing to think or act differently. In essence, "Play better!"

MOVING BEYOND ADVICE

We need more than advice. We need transformation! So I have identified a game changer that can change our whole attitude about protecting ourselves. It helps us develop a different lifestyle, giving us the courage to apply some of the loving solutions from section 1. Maybe it will go way beyond, "Play better!" I certainly hope so.

> Reader: So exactly whose attitude are you saying needs changing? I know you've pointed out some games I've been playing, and I've considered which ones I plan to stop playing. I assume by your comment that you think my overall attitude needs to change, too. That's more than I signed up for.
>
> Joe: Well, here's what I'm thinking. I just set out this vision for you, a vision of what it looks like to live authentically and lovingly with

others—empathetic, self-aware, and transparent. But why would you want to risk the pain of living that way, unless you change your perspective about life?

Reader: I remember you saying that some of your loving solutions could be risky. I guess I just planned to minimize that risk by choosing the games I will stop playing. You know if I'm twenty pounds overweight, I can improve my health by getting rid of some unhealthy foods and lose five pounds—that seems good enough. I can do the same with your games—selectively choose what games to eliminate and I will still be better off.

Joe: As I recall, those diet counselors also say your lifestyle has to change to really improve your health. Those who plan to take the easy way out and just lose five pounds often end up regaining those five pounds. To sustain an authentically loving lifestyle, you probably need to develop an attitude where you can let go of the outcome and stop playing all your games, not just some of them. At least that's my opinion.

So give me a chance with this attitude-adjustment idea. I'm going to start with a different vision—not a vision of authentic living, but instead a vision of controlling my destiny. It's one I have contemplated for several years. It's all part of Step No. 1 for Letting Go.

LETTING GO: STEP NO. 1—STOP TRYING TO CONTROL THE UNCONTROLLABLE

I have had this other vision for some time—not the kind of vision that comes in the middle of the night where you don't know if you are awake or asleep, but more of a picture, an analogy, of how I naturally live my life.

When I look out to the left side of my vision, I am on a hilltop, peering over a sunny meadow that extends for miles. The fields are lush with green grasses and plants, but the trees are not so large that they hinder my view. The hills are rolling, and they greet the horizon just as they grow into mountains. It's a clear, comfortable view of where I am going.

I can't see nearly as well on the right side, because it is enveloped by a heavy fog. I assume the same landscape (the hills rolling into the distance) exists beneath the fog, but I really don't know. I can't see more than thirty feet into the fog. Separating the sunny side from the foggy side is a wooden rail fence that is short enough for me to straddle without hurting myself. Actually, I know it is short enough for me to straddle, because that is exactly what I am doing. I have one foot on the sunny side and one foot on the foggy side, and I am making my way down the hill into the meadow.

I think this is how I live my life, straddling the fence, walking between two different worlds, without committing completely to either side. I prefer the sunny side, where I feel like I am in control. I can see well enough to maneuver my way through the meadow. I can plan my steps and work out the best strategy to make my life journey safe and enjoyable. I am tempted to stop straddling the fence and walk only on the sunny side, avoiding the fog completely.

I don't really like the foggy side, because I don't feel in control at all. It doesn't feel safe. I definitely can't see where I am going. Yet I feel called to it. Maybe it's a call to adventure or a call to faith—I'm not sure. In my heart I actually believe I should be walking down the right side in that fog, trusting God and not trying to control so many things.

At times, I wonder if the power and control I feel on the sunny side are actually a hoax, where I only think I am in control. Do I really have no more control on the sunny side than I do on the foggy side? In real life, these are the times when someone unexpectedly dies or when a tornado levels a neighborhood or when someone at work is unfairly laid off or when a friend's son commits suicide or when I consider my inevitable physical death. I wonder if the feelings I have about the foggy side—the recognition that I can't control the outcome, the gut-wrenching adventure of walking into the unknown, the underlying need to trust God throughout the journey—I wonder if these feelings are more real than the sunny-side feelings of planning and control. I wonder if the foggy side defines life as it really exists. While I wish for the feeling of certainty and safety on the sunny side, I have this nagging awareness that striving to control my journey (even in the sun) is just an illusion.

Actually, the sunny side may have the same potential dangers as the foggy side. I somehow think that if I can plan ahead on the sunny side, I have a better chance of filling my life with good things like comfort, and avoiding bad things like pain. I want to believe that planning ahead makes a difference, even when I am confronted with evidence (cancer, conflict, injustice, or death, for example) that challenges my ability to control my destiny. I finally yield that I cannot control everything. Some parts of my life, actually the most important aspects of my life, are outside my control.

> Reader: Okay. I understand you. As hard as I try, there are major aspects of life that are outside my control, including my death. Thanks for the morbid reminder. Well, that still leaves me in control of the rest. And using your analogy, as I walk on the sunny side, I increase my odds of living comfortably as I plan out (maneuver or manipulate if I have to) how to make life work to my advantage.
>
> Joe: Kind of like your strategies are earning you the good things you experience.
>
> Reader: Of course. That's what planning is all about. You plan your work and work your plan. That's the formula for success, or at least the formula to improve my odds of having a good life. No assurance it will work, but I sure have a better chance of achieving my goals if I plan out my strategy.
>
> Joe: I think I've heard that idea. Larry Crabb says that idea is a popular (but dangerous) way of thinking, "To make life work, trust only yourself and what you can control."[1] By the way, how does all that planning make you feel? No need to answer that question until we get into Step No. 2.

LETTING GO: STEP NO. 2—JUMP TO THE WORST-CASE SCENARIO

I'm not sure about you, but I can tell you how I feel. It takes a lot of effort to live on the sunny side, where my success depends on me. Since I believe that I achieve the good things in my life, I can feel the pressure to ensure my comforts are not replaced by pain. This seems especially true for me when my efforts to plan ahead don't seem to make any difference. I feel more pressure, so I resort to manipulating others, playing my games to get what I want, to the potential disadvantage of others.

Maybe you have felt this way, too. "You've felt the shallowness and pressure of life for a long time. The pleasures you experience don't seem to reach all the way into your soul. They leave you empty and under

---

1. Crabb, *Shattered Dreams*, 18.

pressure to keep them coming. You feel like Atlas holding the world on your shoulders, but your shoulders are not as broad."[2]

It's hard for me to juggle all these efforts, especially when I am trying to hide the fact that I'm serving myself. I want to appear loving and caring, when I'm really planning/scheming to acquire what I think is good for me—not just good material things, but other good things like respect, praise, acceptance, friendships, and feeling good about myself and my accomplishments. It's not easy to line up everyone's opinions and behaviors so they fall in line with my expectations, producing the good-for-me outcome I want. Let's look at some examples:[BL 1-4]

- Situation A—Ivan, the sales consultant. "I have sales goals as a consultant. I am being judged on how well I achieve a good outcome. My pay, my job, my family's income, etc., depend on how well I hit the sales goal—the "good" outcome I am shooting for. When I am calling on a prospect, I can feel the pressure of how critical it is for me to do things right, so I get this sale. That urgency to get the sale can lead me to play games, to not really be honest with others. Maybe the prospect really wouldn't be better off hiring us, but I don't want to admit that to the prospect, because that would put my sales goal at risk. Once the sale is made, the pressure to control the outcome isn't over—it's now critical to my preferred outcome that I get as much internal sales credit as possible, while still looking like a team player. So I negotiate/manipulate the internal sales credit with my fellow team members, to be sure I get as much credit as I can justify, while trying to still appear fair to the team."

- Situation B—Lona, the single parent. "I have a teenager, Jamie, who is skipping school with his friends. We know he is using marijuana frequently, and he sees nothing wrong with it. A high school diploma is important to me, so I feel the pressure to get him through high school. How will he get a decent job without a diploma? Then he gets arrested for dealing drugs—now I feel the pressure that he not be convicted, because we all know that he will have trouble getting a job later if he has a drug conviction on his record. I am trying to control several outcomes, which leads me to enabling his destructive behaviors. I try to manipulate his teachers to pass him, I try to bribe him to study, and I hire a lawyer to

2. Crabb, *The Pressure's Off*, 147.

fight his drug conviction. I am stressed out trying to make sure he will be employable. The pressure is unbearable!"

- Situation C—Cora, the abused wife. "I have a husband who is verbally abusive, but only when no one else is around. Sure, he is controlling and a little bit of a jerk when we are around our friends, but they don't see how bad it really is. That's just the way he is, and sometimes I think I cause him to be mean. My parents would freak out if they knew I just want to leave him, get out of here, and go anywhere but here. Mom never liked him anyway, and I can just hear it, "Told you so." Divorce is so unheard of in our family. Everyone else has a good marriage—I have to make this work. The pressure is on—my marriage can't fail."

- Situation D—Carlos, the hard-working husband. "I work hard all day at my job. When I get home, I deserve time to myself—surf the Internet, check out my Facebook page, get my dinner, and then watch my favorite television shows. I already know the shows I want to watch each evening. I have my schedule down pat. My biggest problem is when my wife wants to start talking about issues from her day, and she can't cover them all during dinner, so her sharing time starts eating (not literally) into the *Jeopardy* television show. How do I get her to hurry up and get through in time? I'm feeling the pressure—what if I miss the entire show? It's not fair. I need my down time. She doesn't have to get up at 5:30 each morning like I do. Why doesn't she understand the pressure she is putting on me?"

I suggest to you that you can use the Worst-Case Scenario Step to relieve some of this pressure. So, let's see how. In each situation, let's imagine what the worst case would look like, if I don't get my preferred outcome. Imagine living in that situation for a few minutes—what does it feel like? Can I actually live with that worst case? Even more important, are there some hidden advantages to me in not getting what I thought I wanted? Let's try the first two situations:

Applying the Worst-Case Scenario to Situation A—
Ivan, the sales consultant

"So what if I don't get this sale? What is the worst case? Well, it could start me on a roll of missing several sales. I could miss my goal for the year. That would be the third year in a row I missed my goal. They could fire me, and then I would have to look for another job. Our family would have to cut back on our standard of living, maybe even sell our house. Wow! I hadn't thought of all the underlying "bad" things I was tying to this one sale. And it's not even clear that any of them will occur, but I am probably subconsciously assuming they will occur. No wonder I feel pressure to manipulate all these people to get this sale and the sales credit!

So what would it look like if the worst event happened—I got fired and had to look for another job? To begin with, I would probably get some severance benefits and then I would be eligible for unemployment. I can see some areas where we could reduce our standard of living and not have to sell our house for several months, maybe even a year. I haven't really liked this job as much as I thought I would anyway, so maybe it wouldn't be so bad to be forced to leave. I actually would have a little more time with the family during the job hunt, which is more time than I have now traveling all over the place to make these sales. Sure, it would be hard to cut back our standard of living, but I think I can see how this might work.

This worst case isn't so bad. I really don't have to mislead this prospect about our product. I can be straight up about the advantages and disadvantages of our product and let them decide whether to buy from us. If I share the pros and cons of my product, the prospect might even give me some extra points for being upfront and honest. I know I would feel better about not hiding our disadvantages. And if we get hired, I really do need to be sure that my fellow team members get credit for all their work. If I really am fair with my team, I bet they would be more willing to support me on another sale in the future.

You know, I think I can live in this place—whether I get the sale or not. I feel freed from the pressure of making this sale. I can just do the best I can, while being upfront and honest. The pressure's off."

Applying the Worst-Case Scenario to Situation B—
Lona, the single parent

So what if Jamie doesn't graduate from high school? I guess he would have to look for a job. I'm not sure he would actually try to get hired. With a drug conviction it would be even harder for him to get hired anyway. He'll probably just hang out at home all day and then go out with his friends at night. I bet he would start dealing drugs to just support himself, because I'm sure not giving him any money. So worst case, I could be stuck with a decision about kicking him out of the house. I'm getting pretty stressed out thinking how bad it could get. Where is his dad when I need him? Now that I think about it, I've already been down this road, thinking about all these terrible consequences. No wonder I'm trying to get him to graduate and to keep the drug conviction off his record. This worst case feels pretty bad.

Okay, so what else do I need to do? Oh yeah, look for the hidden advantages in not getting what I want. So what are the hidden advantages if we go down this road and I end up having to kick Jamie out of the house? I would feel guilty that I wasn't a good enough mom, and now it's obvious to everyone. I guess he would have to actually endure the consequences of his drug use and his lack of focus on his school work. I think I heard that some kids have to "hit bottom" before they actually start making better decisions. Maybe if he had to figure out where to find food and shelter, that would kick-start him into making more responsible decisions. Maybe he would actually consider getting treatment for his drug problem. Or maybe he would die on the streets. I actually wonder if I'm watching him die slowly now—he certainly isn't the same Jamie I knew two years ago. I know I would worry about him and what he was doing, but I already worry about him now. Would it be any worse?

Without Jamie here, I wouldn't have to watch him self-destruct. That is so hard to watch. The tension in our house would be reduced, too. I feel like I walk on eggshells to keep from ticking him off. So do his younger sisters. Who knows, my relationship with Jamie might even be better if he lived outside my house. You know, I could also give his sisters more attention. I sure have been neglecting them. And it would certainly cost me less time and money, if he were on his own.

Well, how about that? There are some advantages to me backing off my efforts to make sure Jamie succeeds. I'm not sure my efforts are working anyway, so maybe manipulating all these people and situations to help Jamie is not what he needs. Oh God, do I have the courage to back off? I actually feel some relief, in the midst of my worries. I think I can live with the worst case. Can I really be freed to make the best decision for me, for Jamie, and for the rest of our family? God, show me what to say and what to do."

Letting Go: Steps 1 and 2: Relieving the Pressure 121

That's what it looks like to jump to the Worst-Case Scenario. It can actually work better if you work through the scenario with someone else, bouncing your ideas off each other. Why don't you try the remaining two situations—Cora and Carlos? Can you use this approach to relieve some of the pressure each one feels? Can you actually feel free to make a loving, authentic decision in each one's situation? Or maybe you may have a situation of your own, already handy, to work through. Give it a shot.

Reader: Okay, so I tried your Worst-Case Scenario. It does seem to be helpful in relieving some of my fears about what could happen if I don't control the situation. But I'm just not sure it works in all situations.

Joe: So, what are you thinking?

Reader: Well, it seems to work best in the sales-consultant situation, where the worst case wasn't so bad. If the worst case is someone could die, like Jamie's son, the Worst-Case Scenario doesn't seem to relieve the pressure very well. It seems to me Jamie was still feeling quite a bit of pressure, even after working through this process.

Joe: I agree. She was dealing with a difficult situation. Her Worst-Case Scenario was awful. And she was feeling all alone. And struggling with self-imposed guilt, leading her to enable Jamie's behavior more than leading her to help Jamie deal with the consequences of his own decisions.

Reader: I think Carlos in Situation D doesn't get much relief from this approach either.

Joe: Why not?

Reader: Off the top, Carlos seems pretty self-centered. Television is more important to him than his wife, and he feels justified in his selfish view. How is he even going to want to live more authentically with his wife? I don't see how the Worst-Case Scenario is going to transform him.

Joe: Good point. He seems to be like Lona's son, Jamie—he needs some earthshaking event to change his view that he has earned the right to do whatever feels best to him. He believes his decision about what is best for him—relaxing his night away in front of the television, the source of his well-earned nightly pleasure—is actually the best for him. He thinks he is exercising his freedom to relax when he is really not free at all. He seems addicted to his television. I can't promise that he will be open to using the next step. I can only say that Step No. 3 seems to offer a better chance of transforming Carlos's attitude.

> **ANOTHER WAY TO USE THE WORST-CASE SCENARIO**
>
> Beth Moore uses a variation of the Worst-Case Scenario to help her let go of her fears. She calls it the "If This, Then _____" process to face any fear:
>
>> Here's what God has been trying to get through to me.... "Beth, it is not enough for you to just trust me, that what you fear most will never happen to you."... [Actually] most of what we fear never does happen to us. Statistics are overwhelming... [however] you and I will never be victorious if this [low probability approach] is the way we approach [our fears]... [because] the enemy will keep threatening us with this fear over and over again....
>>
>> Think about the thing you would dread most, "If that happens, then____." I'm going to wish I was dead. I'll never get up again. My life would never be worth anything anymore. I would never laugh again. I'll never be okay again.... If your worst fear is that your sixteen year-old is not going to make it home tonight, you will lie in bed... and all you can think about over and over is something might happen to that sixteen year-old.... It is a constant threat even though it has not happened....
>>
>> Just before my most recent birthday... [I went through this process with one of my fears] What if [my husband] isn't attracted to me anymore?... What if he starts wanting somebody else?... What if it does happen? Then we've had it. We've said, "God is good, if he does what I say." My faith is completely conditional, because I've said, "I trust you not to let this happen." But what if it does?... God began to teach me, "You're going to have to trust me, period. Trust me—not trust me not to let it happen. Trust me!"...
>>
>> God said to me "Face the fear.... I want you to think that whole thing through—your worst case scenario...." [My] worst-case scenario is that she's young and darling and [my husband] is not just attracted to her, but he falls in love with her. He says to me, "I can't help it. I don't love you anymore. I am in love with her." Worst-case scenario, Lord, my children like her.... Is that a worst-case scenario or what? My children like her....
>>
>> Then what?... Well, I'll be devastated.
>>
>> Okay, then what? I'll have a fit... a long fit.

> Then what? Then I'm probably going to start lying in the floor with a Bible on my head.
> Then what? Well, I'm probably going to have to memorize some Scripture because I won't get through it if I don't....
> Then what? Then one day I'd get up and go back to ministry. I'd be mad as a hornet for a while, taking it out on everybody coming to class. And then I'd get up, because my God is good. He is faithful.
> I know this is hard. I'm not having much ... fun [working my fear through this process]. I'm just saying ... I've been doing this for about fourteen months and I feel like a different person, because now every time it occurs to me ... "What if I lose somebody that I can't live without?" I will lie in the floor and writhe in pain. It's going to kill me, but it will not, because my God is faithful. . . . Should that which I fear most come upon me . . . then my God will take care of me. Anything less than that leaves you in a grip of fear. . . . You've got to know, "If this, then God."
> ... Even if it becomes a reality, I've got to know my God will be faithful to me.[3]
>
> Beth Moore has a good point. Wherever you go with your Worst-Case Scenario, can you picture God there with you? Can you picture God being faithful to you through the pain or will you just blame God (or someone else) for the pain? Or, maybe you'll do both at the same time. Hopefully, your trust in God wins out—that is the place of comfort and peace and freedom—freedom to authentically reach out to care about others in the midst of your own pain. Try it: "If this, then God!"

---

3. Moore, *If You Remain Silent*, Session 4. Reprinted and used by permission.

11

Letting Go: Steps 3 and 4: Experiencing the Freedom

So far, we have admitted some things are out of our control (Step No. 1). Then we took some of the pressure off by learning how to jump to the Worst Case Scenario (Step No. 2). Now we are going to replace that pressure with a sense of freedom, after we work through the last two steps of this chapter. To make the leap into fully letting go of the outcome, we will address a potential issue with the Worst Case Scenario.

My friend Laney explains how she used to "pre-disasterize" many events in her life, by imagining the upcoming disaster. It's like she was going to the "dark side" of the Worst Case Scenario. She would think through how bad the situation might turn out and then worry about all the potentially "bad" consequences. Instead of seeing that she could live with the worst case or seeing that God would be there with her if disaster occurred, Laney fretted about how "bad" it was going to be.

I wonder how Laney determined which possible consequence was going to be "bad." This seems so obvious, doesn't it? Good things feel good and bad things hurt, right? But is it really that clear? How about you—have you ever wondered about your definition of "good" vs. "bad"? Hopefully the next step will help you sort out some answers to this apparently obvious question.

LETTING GO: STEP NO. 3—WE REALLY DON'T KNOW WHAT IS GOOD FOR US

In William Young's bestselling novel, *The Shack*, Mack works through his pain and anger toward God through several conversations with God at the shack. One conversation with Sarayu (an epiphany of the Holy Spirit) matches up well with our innate desire to control our lives so they are more comfortable:

> [Sarayu speaks to Mack,] "When something happens to you, how do you determine whether it is good or evil?"
>
> Mack thought for a moment before answering. "Well, I haven't really thought about that. I guess I would say something is good when I like it—when it makes me feel good or gives me a sense of security. Conversely, I'd call something evil that causes me pain or costs me something I want."
>
> "So it is pretty subjective then?"
>
> "I guess it is."
>
> "And how confident are you in your ability to discern what indeed is good for you, or what is evil?"
>
> "To be honest," said Mack, ". . . I'm not really sure I have any logical ground for deciding what is actually good or evil, except how something or someone affects me." He paused to rest and catch his breath a moment. "All seems quite self-serving and self-centered, I suppose. And my track record isn't very encouraging either. Some things I initially thought were good turned out to be horribly destructive and some things that I thought were evil, well, they turned out [good]. . . .
>
> "I can see now," confessed Mack, "that I spend most of my time and energy trying to acquire what I have determined to be good, whether it's financial security or health or retirement or whatever. And I spend a huge amount of energy and worry fearing what I've determined to be evil." Mack sighed deeply.
>
> "Such truth in that," said Sarayu gently. "Remember this. It allows you to play God in your independence. . . . You must give up your right to decide what is good and evil on your own terms."[1]

Wow! Did you catch all that? We have this inherent desire to "plan our work and work our plan," so we can achieve good things and avoid pain in our lives. Yet, we are only guessing that the good things we crave will actually be good for us. And we are only guessing that the bad or painful things we want to avoid will actually be bad for us.

Like Carlos in Situation D, we assume that our equivalent to his nightly television ritual, the one he has earned and one that he craves for relaxation, is actually the best thing for us. It sounds like another version of the ESP Game—we're just speculating about things we don't

1. Young, *The Shack*, 134–136.

understand at all. Then acting as if we know our speculations are true, we do what Mack confessed—we spend most of our time and energy to acquire what we think is good for us and to avoid what we think is bad for us.

An ancient Taoist story converts this philosophy into day-to-day life:

> A farmer ... used an old horse to till his fields. One day, the horse escaped into the hills and when the farmer's neighbors sympathized with the old man over his bad luck, the farmer replied, "Bad luck? Good luck? Who knows?"
>
> A week later, the horse returned with a herd of horses from the hills and this time the neighbors congratulated the farmer on his good luck. His reply was, "Good luck? Bad luck? Who knows?"
>
> Then, when the farmer's son was attempting to tame one of the wild horses, he fell off its back and broke his leg. Everyone thought this very bad luck. Not the farmer, whose only reaction was, "Bad luck? Good luck? Who knows?"
>
> Some weeks later, the army marched into the village and conscripted every able-bodied youth they found there. When they saw the farmer's son with his broken leg, they let him off. Now was that good luck or bad luck? Who knows?[2]

If, like this farmer, we don't really know what is good for us versus what is bad for us, what is the use in trying to control our circumstances and control other people, just to manipulate them into serving our perception of our needs? Larry Crabb goes a step further, explaining how painful moments in our lives are actually a part of God's journey for us:

> *God wants to bless us.* . . . Because he can't resist giving us the highest good, he's determined to give us an encounter with himself. It's the greatest blessing he can think of. . . .
>
> *The deepest pleasure we're capable of experiencing is an encounter with God.* . . . [But] we have our own ideas about what a good God should do in the middle of our circumstances, ideas that stretch all the way from opening a space in a crowded parking lot . . . to straightening out our kids to giving us a negative biopsy report. . . . We almost always mistake lesser pleasures for this greatest pleasure and live our lives chasing after . . . [these] lower dreams . . . [of] enough health and money to enjoy life. . . . The greatest dream [of encountering God] is available. But we don't view things that way.

---

2 "Good Luck Bad Luck!"

So God goes to work to help us see more clearly. One way [but not the only way] he works is to allow our lower dreams to shatter. He lets us hurt and doesn't make it better. . . . In fact, what he's doing while we suffer is leading us into the depths of our being, into the center of our soul where we feel our strongest passions. It's there we discover our desire for God . . . a desire to know him that not only survives all our pain, but actually thrives in it. Through the pain of shattered lower dreams, we wake up to the realization that we want an encounter with God [the greatest dream], more than we want the blessings of life.

And that begins a revolution in our lives. . . . *Our shattered dreams are never random. They are always a piece in a larger puzzle, a chapter in a larger story.* Pain is a tragedy. But it's never only a tragedy. For the Christian, it's always a necessary mile on the long journey to joy . . . . Shattered dreams are . . . ordained opportunities for the spirit [of God] first to awaken and then to satisfy our highest dream [of encountering God] . . . .

[So let's] interpret all of life's hardships not as problems to fix or struggles to relieve or pain to deaden, but as important elements in a larger story. . . . Accept wherever [we] are on the journey, whether happy or miserable, as the place where God will meet [us], where he loves [us], where he will continue to work in [us]. . . .

In the middle of our shattered dreams, Jesus is restraining himself, for reasons we cannot fully understand, from ending our pain. . . . As the mother holds her baby still so the doctor can deliver the needed injection, so [our] Lord is allowing [us] to suffer for reasons [we] do not know. . . . [Here's the] mystery . . . it's more difficult for Christ to restrain himself from making all our dreams come true than for us to watch them shatter. At our moment of worst pain, Jesus' pain is worse.[3]

Willard "Ouija" Sink, founder of the Parakaleo ministry, summarizes his experience of shattered dreams: "Earlier in my life I heard, 'God loves you and has a wonderful plan for your life.' Now I believe, 'God loves you and he will wreck your life until you are broken—and he's wonderful.'" Ouija has not only accepted his life journey, as hard and painful as it has been, but he now celebrates God's work in his life. He is daily loving and letting go of the outcome.

How does all this philosophy play out in real life? Recently Sherri, one of the parents in our support group was sharing her journey with the rest of us, after years of turmoil dealing with her son's drug addiction. "I

---

3. Crabb, *Shattered Dreams*, 2–5, 81, 116, 119.

used to try to control everything connected with my son—his addiction, his recovery, his relapse, his relationships, and so on. There was so much pressure to get him and everyone else to fall in line and act right. Then I realized all this was outside my control [Step No. 1 for Letting Go]. I also realized that I didn't even know what was best for our son, even if I could have controlled all this stuff [Step No. 3 for Letting Go]."

So where are we in our attitude adjustment? I think Sherri hit on it:

- Some of this stuff is really outside our control.
- When we try to manipulate others to try to control the controllable, we feel the pressure to make it work.
- While Sherri didn't mention the Worst-Case Scenario, we can relieve some of the pressure by realizing that the worst thing that could happen may not be so bad after all.
- Even with that thought, I realize that I really don't know it all. I don't even know if the stuff I can control will lead to results that are actually good for me. My short-term assumption is comfort is good and pain is bad, but that is not necessarily true. God works through pain, too.

> **WHAT ARE YOU TRYING TO CONTROL?**
>
> It took Sherri several years to identify the area of her life she was trying to control. How can you shortcut that process? Dwight Edwards thinks you try to control areas of your life that feed your natural identity. You're doing it without even thinking about it—it's so natural. In case you want to discover your area of control, you could just ask a relative or close friend. I suspect he or she sees it pretty clearly. Or you could follow Edwards' suggestion:
>
>> Here's a test. Ask yourself, 'What role, responsibility, or aspect of my life has the potential to trigger in me the deepest disappointment as well as the highest happiness?' If you're a parent [like Sherri] it might be your children's behavior more than anything else that can cause you either to soar with pride or die of embarrassment. If so, your primary identity label is probably that of a mother or father. Your children's conduct then becomes the real barometer of your personal worth and significance, and you may find yourself trying to control your children rather than releasing them in God's direction.[4]

4. Edwards, *Revolution*, 101.

> Applying this to myself, I think some of my greatest disappointments are the times when I disappoint a client, while some of my greatest feelings of achievement come from helping a client in some creative way. And now that I think about it, that is an area where I do try to control how I come across. I think through what that client will think if I say this or do that. I'm learning to release these situations to God, too, although it is hard to not intervene to be sure my team delivers the best service, even if it means sacrificing my family or other "more valuable" aspects of my life. I definitely feel the pressure to perform with my work, to try to control the outcome.

Reader: Hold on! This is a pretty big leap for me. You think I don't know what's good or bad for me. Well, here's what I think—I see the logic from *The Shack* (kind of Philosophy 101 or something) and I even get the point of that story about the farmer, but I don't normally think like that. At least I like Larry Crabb's honesty—he admits these shattered dreams are painful. I know I can distinguish what is comfortable from what is painful, and I sure prefer comfort over pain, even if it is a short-term result. You're asking me to not try to avoid the pain, that the pain may be necessary for me to attain something greater.

Joe: That's why letting go of the outcome is an attitude adjustment, a change in your perspective. It's difficult to think that something painful may actually be good for you. It won't be easy to change the way you look at the world. After all, you've been thinking this way for years, right?

Reader: Sure, who doesn't think this way? Maybe Mother Teresa or that ancient farmer or that Larry Crabb guy when he's selling his books. I'm just a normal person trying to support myself and my family. If I really don't know what's good for me, why do I even try to work hard or make any plans at all? If I'm letting go of the outcome, I now feel like letting go altogether. What's the use?

Joe: I thought you'd never ask. That brings us to Step No. 4 for Letting Go—experiencing the freedom and joy of living out of love for others.

LETTING GO: STEP NO. 4—FEEL THE FREEDOM OF JUST LOVING OTHERS

So let's review the process so far:

- While I theoretically see that loving others is the most rewarding way to live, I end up trying to protect myself to ensure my comfort and avoid pain. I sabotage my own efforts to be kind, patient, forgiving, courteous, humble, generous, and honest, when I feel I have to fend off real or perceived personal threats.

- Protecting myself against these threats leads me to play various relationship games that are manipulative, unloving, and dishonest. I may play them subconsciously, not even recognizing these games, at least not recognizing them until I read this book. Or maybe I did recognize some of them, but I just didn't see how harmful they were to my relationships. I definitely didn't notice that I was sending out unintended messages that keep the games from working to my advantage.

- I have been given some loving solutions to these games and a start on what my life would look like if I lived more authentically and more lovingly. This game changer, intended to change my perspective, is to let go of the outcome. Like the Taoist farmer, I don't know enough about the past, present, or future to know if trying to control the events in my life and manipulating others will ultimately end up giving me more comfort or more pain.

- If we don't spend all our energy trying to acquire what we think is good and avoid what we think is bad, what are we going to do with our energy? If we can't be reasonably sure that our efforts will be rewarded with good things we have earned, why should we even try? What is this freedom I'm supposed to be feeling—maybe that will make a difference?

Most of us think of freedom as being "free" to do what I want to do. No restrictions. No rules. Just meeting my wants and needs and even my passions, whatever they are. It sounds so selfish, doesn't it? In their book, *Judaism for Dummies* (nice title, huh?), Rabbi Ted Falcon and David Blatner offer their view of choosing freedom from our fears and other areas that control our lives:

Everyone loves the freedom to do stuff . . . to go places, to see and do what we want. . . . The "freedom to" is obviously extremely important, but some say the "freedom from" is even more precious. As Dr. Avram Davis writes, "To be free from anger, free from hatred, free from chains that bind the heart . . . This is what it means to be free."

. . . If every time you visit your parents, you turn into a fourteen-year-old kid inside, you are not free. If you just "have" to have the newest, hottest gadget as soon as it hits the market, you're not free. You may be free to do anything you want, but if you are a slave to television, or the stock market, or getting your way, you're not free . . .[5]

What if I'm "free from" the slavery of trying to control the outcome and so I'm now "free to" fulfill my God-given passion, the loving purpose for my life that he has instilled deep in me? It seems that I am back at the introduction of this book, but now I have the ability to overcome the desire to protect myself. I might as well try to live a personally satisfying life of love, if I can't ensure that the preferred outcome of my efforts is actually "good" for me.

I think I just need to make this theory of loving others a reality in my life:

- Stop giving in to my fears. Stop being dishonest and controlling. Give up the pressure that I feel in that lifestyle.

- Trade that pressure for the freedom I feel when I really care about others—free to be kind, patient, forgiving, courteous, humble, generous, and honest.[6] I am free to live out the vision of authentic relationships—self-aware, transparent, and empathetic while letting go of the outcome.

- When I have nothing to hide or defend, I am free to just act out of love, to love others as unconditionally as God loves me.

- My perspective on life changes. This is not fatalism, just letting life happen to me. Instead, as I am freed to love others, what I once considered to be an overbearing responsibility is now a wonderful *privilege*. What I once considered to be a painful journey to be endured is now an *opportunity* to see God work.

5. Falcon and Blatner, *Judaism*, 297.
6. Chapman, *Love as a Way of Life*, 5.

Ultimately, this freedom to let go of the outcome, the freedom to not protect myself, the freedom not to manipulate others, comes from trust. I have to be willing to trust God with whatever direction my life takes. Rather than trying to make my life work to my advantage (and playing games to force that advantage), I trust God to be with me on my journey. I listen to his voice directing me to make decisions out of love (sometimes even out of "tough love").

I like the way Papa and Sarayu (two manifestations of God) explain this to Mack in *The Shack*: "We [God] created you, the human, to be in a face-to-face relationship with us, to join our circle of love. . . . If you knew that I [God's spirit] was good and that everything—the means, the ends, and all the processes of individual lives—is all covered by my goodness, then while you might not always understand what I am doing, you will trust me. . . . Trust is the fruit of a relationship in which you know you are loved."[7]

As my wife, Beth, says, you can only give what you have. As I know and experience God's love, I can give that same love back to God and to other people. I have no pressure on me, because God loves and accepts me, even when I mess up. I know and experience that I am loved by God and I can give that same love to others in complete freedom and joy.

Here's a real-life example of letting go and acting out of love, without manipulating the situation. Some friends are reading through this book with me, as a test to see if these game concepts and other ideas actually make sense. We are trying to apply one of the reading hints in the Introduction—we are meeting weekly and discussing our games and ways we can be more loving. Ned, a financial advisor, is a member of this group. He shared a story about himself that illustrates the freedom that comes from letting go of the outcome:

> Recently, a client called me and accused me of misleading him about a withdrawal from his account. It turns out he owed taxes on the transaction, which was a surprise to both of us. I could tell he was angry, especially when he blurted out, "How can you call yourself a financial advisor?"
>
> We could have argued about whose fault it was—I actually think we each had a share of the blame. But I just let it go. [He didn't play the Blame Game, at least not that long.] After I got off the phone, his comments echoed in my brain. I couldn't con-

---

7. Young, *The Shack*, 124, 126.

centrate on anything else. He was a client and a friend, and I was afraid I was going to lose both relationships.

I checked back over the information I had, to see how I would have known he would owe taxes on this deal. When I couldn't find any source that would have shown me it was taxable, I wondered what I could say to him, to justify my actions, to prove that I really was competent.

I got into my car and drove to his office. The anxiety was unbearable. What was I going to say? Would it heal our relationship or would I lose a friend? I decided on the drive over to just apologize for my part and let it go at that. No guarantee how he would respond.

It's a funny thing—as I was standing in front of him and apologizing, I stopped feeling anxious. I actually felt relieved [free]. I wasn't relieved when it was over—I started feeling relieved as I was speaking. I could not tell what he would say or do, but I no longer was trying to control the outcome. I was just doing what I thought was right.

Now, that's what I'm talking about. Ned was acting out of love, without regard to the outcome. His initial anxiety and fears actually changed to a sense of relief and freedom, as he shared honestly and humbly with his client friend. In this case, his friend accepted his apology and their relationship was restored. There was no assurance of that outcome—Ned could not control his friend's response. He could only act out of love and let go of the result, experiencing a sense of freedom during the process.

Let's summarize the transforming steps that help us let go of the outcome:

- Stop trying to control the uncontrollable. It's a foggy world of unknowns out there, no matter how much we plan our work and work our plan. Trying to control the uncontrollable aspects of our lives ultimately leads to frustration and despair.
- Walk through the Worst-Case Scenario. We can let go of our fears more easily when we work through what life could look like if the worst case actually occurred. Sometimes we realize that the worst case isn't so bad, and other times we realize that it appears to be awful, yet we will figure out how to cope with it.
- We really don't know what's good for us. We can yield control of the outcome as we recognize that our obvious desire for comfort and our avoidance of pain may not provide the best results for us.

We have to challenge our inbred assumptions about what is good and what is bad to take advantage of this game changer.

- Trade the pressure of making things work for the freedom and joy of loving others. Not only is letting go of the outcome logical and loving, it actually feels more freeing. This is not a coping mechanism to deal with your stress, but it is a release of your issues to God. Why not choose to feel free and at peace?

So do you buy this approach? How did this game changer work for you? Can you actually make the leap to let go of the outcome? Can you trust a loving God to be with you as you leap into loving others, no matter the results?

When I actually follow through with it, letting go has transformed my attitude about life. For me, I try to do my best and leave the results to God, trusting that his journey for me (however fun or painful it may seem) is exactly the journey that is best. He has a greater story, and I am only a part of that story, definitely not the central part. I truly want to fulfill his designated role for me in his greater story and I don't want to get distracted by my need to address my fears and protect myself.

I believe that I fulfill my designed role when I am authentic and loving. Letting go of the outcome certainly makes it easier to live that way. I don't have to worry about others taking advantage of me. I can relax in my relationships. Instead of trying to convince others to not vote me off the lifeboat, I can actually try to help them with compassion. It also makes it easier for me to take the other steps as an authentic lover—to become more self-aware, transparent, and empathetic.

> **LETTING GO DURING A FAMILY CRISIS**
>
> Like Ned, Beth and I have felt the freedom of letting go of the outcome. Beth recorded this reflection during a critical period with our son's drug abuse:
>
>> *Then God said, "Take your son, your only son, Isaac, whom you love, and go to the region of Moriah. Sacrifice him there as a burnt offering on one of the mountains I will tell you about. . . . Do not lay a hand on the boy. Do not do anything to him. Now I know you fear God, because you have not withheld from me your son, your only son"(Gen 22:2, 12 NIV).*
>>
>> We had done everything we knew to do. There had been three treatment programs, two halfway houses, counseling, begging,

> pleading, and praying. . . . [Our son] had spiraled out again. A call from his counselor at the halfway house informed us they had kicked him out of the house because of drugs . . . *again!*
>
> They were "done" . . . we were "done." [Our son] was on the streets.
>
> I felt God speak to my heart through the Scripture above, "Give me your son. He is not alone. I am with him."
>
> Letting go is a process. I knew letting him go and giving God my son was the only thing left. I thought I had released him to God. But this was one more time he was asking me to give him my son. I knew what he meant. He meant not only give him my son—he meant give him the outcome. Turn over to him all that could and might happen to [our son].
>
> But what will that mean? Will [he] live or die? Death was a real possibility.[8]
>
> For both Beth and me, letting go of our fears and our desires to control our son were turning points during this family crisis. You can see why Letting Go is such an important game changer in our lives, helping us live when death seemed imminent.
>
> It took us awhile to get there when our son was struggling with drug addiction. And it could take us awhile again, depending on what's going on in our lives at the time. If it does take awhile next time, it just means we will be retaining a delusion of control, along with its feeling of pressure, while delaying that sense of freedom when we let go of the outcome.

---

8. Lineberry and Lineberry, *"Give Me Your Son" and Other Reflections*, 4.

Section Three

Where Is God in All This?

12

God's Work as the Ultimate Game Changer

WE HAVE UNCOVERED GAMES which cripple our relationships, and we have reviewed some loving solutions to replace our games. Then we considered a major game changer, Letting Go of the Outcome, which frees us from our self-focused attitude so we can concentrate on loving others. It's a fair question—where is God in all this? More specifically, what is God's view of our games? Does he endorse this vision of authentic living? And what's his role in improving our relationships with each other?

WHERE DO AUTHENTIC RELATIONSHIPS FALL ON GOD'S PRIORITY LIST?

It appears obvious to me that God is in the business of authentic relationships, especially reconciling our relationships through his love:

- In the Old Testament, Moses, Ezekiel, and Daniel all talk about God's provisions for reconciliation for us (Lev 8:15, Ezek 45:15–17, Dan 9:24). Judaism devotes forty consecutive days each year to repentance and reconciliation with each other and with God during their holy days of Rosh Hashanah and Yom Kippur. According to New Testament writer Paul, God has taken the initiative to reconcile us to himself through Christ, and then he has asked us to join him in this message and work of reconciliation for others (2 Cor 5:18–19, Eph 2:13–18).

- Jesus affirmed that the greatest commandments are to love God with all our heart and to love our neighbors as ourselves (Matt 22:36–40). Then Jesus took God's laws to another level when he insisted that loving thoughts and attitudes were the key, not just our actions (Matt 5–7, Mark 7:20–23). He even instructed us to love our enemies (Matt 5:43–48). How radical is that!

- Jan Johnson points out that Jesus didn't play games (and she hadn't even read this book). His "authenticity . . . showed in how people never had to wonder what he was up to. . . . Jesus was not phony, hypocritical, flattering, sanctimonious, counterfeit, deceptive, or misleading. He could be counted on not to scheme or design, connive or manipulate, or change his manner around certain people . . . [unlike our current society] he used *things* and loved *people*."[1] In one of his early church letters, Paul even cast a vote for authentic living when he wrote, "We refuse to wear masks and play games. We don't manipulate and maneuver behind the scenes. And we don't twist God's word to suit ourselves. Rather we keep everything we do and say out in the open, the whole truth on display" (2 Cor 4:2 MSG)

- Throughout the Bible we are given this vision of authentic living—letting go of the outcome (Job 1: 21–22, Hab 3:17–19, Phil 4:6–7, 11–13), self-awareness (Lam 3:40, 2 Cor 13:5–6, Gal 6:4, Eph 5:15–17), transparency (Zech 8:16–17, Eph 4:15, Col 3:9, James 5:16), and compassionate empathy (2 Cor 1:3–4, 11:29, Gal 6:2, 1 Pet 3:8–9). I believe that many of the loving solutions are twenty-first century applications of biblical truths. So this really isn't my vision of loving relationships and authentic living—this vision and these game changers seem to come from God.

In summary, I believe with my head and my heart that God is at work in us to build honest and loving relationships. I hope this book actually helps you and me to fulfill our call to reconciliation and loving one another.

So it's not-so-breaking news. This vision of authentic living *is* God's business! God is all about relationships. To put it differently, God is the ultimate relationship. Jan Johnson points out that Jesus is "one of a three-person community of love . . . [and] relating in such community is the eternal kind of life we were built for."[2]

---

1. Johnson, *Invitation*, 60–61.
2. Ibid., 31.

Until recently, I had always thought of God, Jesus Christ, and the Holy Spirit as functional roles of God—that is, each one had a specific role to fill as part of the Trinity:

- God is the Father, the Godhead—in my view of the hierarchy, God is number one.
- Jesus is that part of God (God's Son) who came to earth to redeem the world and us from our sinful nature.
- The Holy Spirit replaced Jesus on earth, because the Holy Spirit can indwell all our hearts, but Jesus' earthly form was more limited by space.

I now see Johnson's point that the Trinity is not just functional, but the Trinity is also relational. William Young's fictional book *The Shack* illustrates the divine relationship in the Trinity. God the Father, Jesus, and the Holy Spirit (as separate persons within the Trinity) have an honest, transparent, loving, even enjoyable relationship with each other.[3] So I wondered, is that what their relationship with each other is actually like? No wonder God created us, since he wanted to share with us that same type of loving relationship. He didn't want to just keep that love within himself—he "enlarged that circle [of love]" to include us.[4] So if God, Jesus, and the Holy Spirit can relate like that, full of authentic love and joy, well that's what I want, too. God invites us to that relationship by reconciling us to himself through Christ. I want to be caught up in that bond of love, and I want to share it with others, too.

HOW DO OUR GAMES MATCH GOD'S VIEW OF LOVE?

Let's flip this conversation to a review of the games we play, contrasted to the model of love described by Paul in his first recorded letter to Corinth (1 Cor 13). Do our games have a place in this circle of love? You may recall God's ideal of love from our vision of being authentic lovers:

> We are patient and kind. We are not jealous of others' success or boastful of our own. We are not puffed up with pride. We live honorably and properly, not rudely or disgracefully. We are not selfish and we do not demand our own way—in essence, we are not self-centered. We are not irritable, and we keep no record

---

3. Young, *The Shack*, 107–108.
4. Johnson, *Invitation*, 31.

of wrongs. We rejoice with the truth. Instead of rejoicing in the misfortune of others, we actually protect them and trust them. We remain hopeful and persevere through all our challenges.[5]

How much do our games prevent us from being this type of godly, authentic lover? Just ponder this question for a moment and see if you agree that our games cripple God's circle of love:

- In our ESP Games, we assume the worst motives of others, rather than protecting them or trusting them. It's almost like we rejoice in speculating about their malicious motives and the causes of their misfortunes.
- In our Don't Change Me Games, we are irritable while demanding our own way—we will not change.
- In our Avoiding Responsibility Games, we typically keep records of how others have wronged us, thus giving us permission to insist on our innocence and ignore the truth.
- In our Isolation Games, we pull back from trusting others and selfishly focus on protecting ourselves.
- In our Be Perfect Like Me Games, we are arrogant and boastful as we try to convince others to think and act like we do.
- In our Passive Be Like Me Games, we are just as arrogant as we keep a record of wrongs and judge others, virtually rejoicing in their misfortunes.
- In our Serve Me Games, we are demanding our own way in an underhanded, manipulative manner, basically tricking others to do what we want.
- In our Looking Good Games, we want to look honorable without being honorable. We are acting out of jealousy, yearning for the praise and honor we see others receiving.

To sum it up, we play these games when we believe "God can't be trusted" (we must take matters into our own hands) and "people don't matter" (we use them to increase our comfort and reduce our pain).[6] What a contradiction to the words of Jesus, "Love God with all your heart and love others as yourselves" (Matt 22: 37–40)! Our relationship

---

5. Morris, *1 Corinthians*, 180–182.
6. Edwards, *Revolution*, 27.

games are all focused on ourselves rather than focused on loving others. When we play these games, they tear down our relationships; however, when we live out of love, we build each other up. I personally prefer being built up, and I bet you do, too.

> **WHAT IF I (THE READER) DON'T BELIEVE IN YOUR GOD?**
>
> I recognize that you may not believe in God or Jesus Christ or the Holy Spirit. You may have a different concept of God, or you may not believe he (or she) exists at all. You may have "tried" some faith called Christianity, and all you can see is how some Christians have let you down, how even God has let you down, how he didn't protect you when you were hurt, how you didn't sense his presence during really painful moments in your life. You may not have noticed at the time, but I believe he was there, trying to comfort you, because he (through Christ) personally knows what pain and rejection feel like. I can only say that God's working through my faith in Christ is bringing me to a place of freedom and love and peace, and I like to live in that place.
>
> At this point, I want to play the ultimate Be Like Me Game. I want you to become like me, letting God reconcile both of us to himself through Christ. For me, it's a matter of eternal life or death. Yet I will listen to my own advice from chapter 5 and let this go. I will trust God to work in your life (and in my life), in ways I cannot even imagine. And I will be there to love you unconditionally, whether you believe like me or not.
>
> My guess is this is a matter of supreme importance to you as well—similarly a matter of eternal life or death. I would love to hear your story of what your God has done in your life, how you have arrived at where you are today. I think stories like these are fascinating. Share your stories with me at http://discuss.exploringpossibilities.net. I would love to hear from you.
>
> Ultimately, what you or I believe about God does not change who God really is or what he desires for us. It really is not "my" God or "your" God. It is really God, as God exists. We are both searching for the same thing—the truth about God and our purpose in this life we have been given. God, I ask you, show us your truth! I look

> forward to the journey God has for each of us (which apparently includes you reading this book).
>
> In my search for God, I found that he was searching for me all along. I studied several religions, all the while trying to find the truth about God. After I concluded Jesus must have resurrected and I gave my heart to Christ, I realized that God had been searching for me all that time that I was searching for him. It still feels that way now—I go off searching for some better understanding of this world, some solution to a personal issue or a friend's issue, and I later feel like God was searching for me the whole time, too. Ironic, isn't it? Or maybe it's just the love of God.
>
> As far as this book goes, it seems to me that many of these principles for living authentically still work, wherever you place your faith—"my" God, "your" God, or someplace else. I can say that in my life, God adds the power and motivation for me to live a transparent life of love, while he reconciles me to him and to other people. I need him, if I am to have any hope of transforming my good intentions into reality.

IS THIS IT—GOD ENDORSES AUTHENTIC RELATIONSHIPS?

We have spent a lot of time in this book cultivating a lifestyle of authentic living:

- Discovering the games we play and why we play them
- Considering loving solutions to playing these games
- Seeking a transformation in our perspective, freeing us to love others with no pressure to control the outcome

Now we have seen that this vision of authentic living (and authentic loving) is consistent with God's principles in the Bible (at least according to my interpretation of the Bible). It even seems to match how he lives and loves us, consistent with the circle of love within the Trinity.

Is that all there is? Is it now up to me to pull this off? Thank God, the answer is "No, it is not just up to you or me!"

A remarkable, inner transformation has taken place among believers, and we really can be the person we've been transformed to be—forsaking our games and living as authentic lovers. God's power is there, his spirit is working within us, comforting and guiding us. Rob Bell explains it this way:

> Paul writes in Colossians, "You have been raised with Christ." I have this new life, this new identity that has been given to me. I have taken on the identity of Christ....
>
> It's not that we are perfect now or that we will never have to struggle. Or that the old person won't come back from time to time. It's that this new way of life involves a constant, conscious decision to keep dying to the old so we can live in the new ... we are literally now a "new creation."
>
> I am being remade.
> I am not who I was.
> I am a new creation.
> I am "in Christ." ...
> And Christ is perfect . . . .
>
> In these passages, we are being told *who we are* now.... This is an issue of identity. It is letting what God says about us shape what we believe about ourselves....
>
> I am not who I was.
> You are not who you were.
> Old person going away. New person here, now.
> Reborn, rebirthed, remade, reconciled, renewed ....
>
> This has huge implications for when I do stumble ... and the old person comes back from the dead for a few moments.
>
> I admit it.
> I confess it.
> I thank God I am forgiven.
> I make amends with anyone who has been affected by my actions.
> And then I move on.
>
> Not because sin isn't serious, but because I am taking seriously who God says I am. The point isn't my failure. It is God's success in remaking me into the person he originally intended me to be.
>
> God's strength, not mine.[7]

Wow! That's the life I want—remade, reconciled, renewed, all through God's strength.

God *is* the Ultimate Game Changer! As Jesus promised his disciples (including me), out of my heart will flow "rivers of living water" (John

---

7. Bell, *Velvet Elvis*, 140–144.

7:38). I just need to release the good (the living water) that God has supernaturally placed in my heart.[8]

Paul reminds us of this truth—we "are the temple of God, and God himself is present in [us]" (1 Cor 3:16 MSG). He is empowering us with his presence in our lives, not with some divine energy bolt from heaven. Not only is God living within us, but Paul explains why there is no reason to play these games—"everything is already [ours] as a gift . . . the world, life, death, the present, the future—all of it is [ours] and [we] are privileged to be in union with Christ, who is in union with God" (1 Cor. 3:21-23 MSG).

How is this true—that we have everything as a gift? It doesn't feel like everything is mine. I must have everything as a gift only as I am in relationship with God and with a worldwide body of believers. As I am united with them, I am experiencing authentic life. I am overflowing with all the gifts they have. What's theirs is mine and what's mine is theirs, as we are connected with each other in love. I really do have it all—there's no need to use manipulative games to get what I already have.

So how does this play out practically in our lives—our inner transformation, releasing the "good" that God has placed in our hearts? Dwight Edwards gives an example:

> We aren't called to figure out new ways to think positively about ourselves, but to humbly and gratefully trust what God says about who we are in Christ. Our true identity . . . ("in Christ," "a new creation" . . . "complete" in Christ . . . "children of God," "heirs of God," "more than conquerors") . . . [is] a gift from God . . . and it's ready now to be applied.
>
> [For example] I just finished making a difficult phone call. It concerned a fairly messy and complicated situation with the potential of becoming ugly, and I felt wholly inadequate to handle it. I dreaded the call and kept putting it off all day.
>
> What helped me most to finally dial the number was reminding myself of what God has placed within me. My inadequacies aren't all there is to me; within me resides *God's very nature* of love, compassion, boldness, and wisdom, and this is actually more central to who I am than any of my shortcomings.
>
> This was my sole hope for handling the call in a God-honoring fashion. I trusted God to provide what I needed to glorify him and to love the person I will be talking with. With genuine reliance on God, I made the call, although still a bit reluctantly.

---

8. Edwards, *Revolution*, 17.

How did it go? Okay. Not great. Not terrible. On the whole I felt I was simply releasing what God had put within me... overall my spoken words and tone seemed like God's doing. I don't know what the results of the call will be, but that's not the issue. I sensed God's flowing, and in that I rest gratefully.[9]

Conner, a friend of mine, shared a similar experience—where he acted out of love, released the good that God had put into his heart and then let go of the outcome. His wife, Jill, had had an affair with another man. Conner and Jill had tried marital counseling, but they could not reconcile their differences. On the night before they were to sign their legal separation papers, Conner felt led by God to go talk with Jill. He felt no love for her. What he felt was anger and hurt and anxiety about their children. In the midst of all those emotions, he told her, "I know we are scheduled to finalize our separation tomorrow. I will tear up these papers right now, and we can start over with another counselor. If you want to make our marriage work, I am willing to do whatever it takes to heal our marriage."

Conner painfully recalls the next few moments, "Jill looked at me with a look of amazement. Then she laughed in my face and walked out of the room. I felt embarrassed and stupid for bringing up this idea. Did I really hear God tell me to do this? I hurt so badly. I was humiliated. Looking back at that moment, I now see what God was doing. I was yielding to his call to love Jill at all costs. I am now comforted that I did everything I could to save our marriage."

That's what I'm talking about. Dwight and Conner were both letting God's love flow through them—letting God work in their relationships, then letting go of the outcome. I can't think of a better way to live.

ARE CHRISTIANS REALLY AUTHENTIC?

David Kinnaman and Gabe Lyons completed some groundbreaking research in 2007 on the opinions of Americans about Christianity. For example, they found that 84 percent of young non-Christians (those under thirty years old) say they know at least one committed Christian, yet only 15 percent of them see that the lifestyles of committed Christians are significantly different from the norm.[10]

---

9. Ibid., 100–101.
10. Kinnamon and Lyons, *UnChristian*, 48.

As we confess our rebellion against God, we know that God loves and saves us. That's not the message others hear. Instead:

> The most common message people hear from us is that Christianity is a religion of rules and regulations . . . [that leads many Christians] to give a false pretense of holiness . . . project[ing] a got-it-together image. We want to make ourselves look as though we have tamed our struggle with sin. [sounds like a Looking Good Game] [A] significant antidote to [this] hypocrisy is . . . transparency. On one level, hypocrisy is failing to acknowledge the inconsistencies in our life. It is denial. . . . Living with integrity starts with being transparent . . . [and Christians really] should have a head start. Transparency simply means admitting what the Bible says about us: We are fallen people who desperately need God in our lives—every day.[11]

According to a less comprehensive survey of "de-churched" Christians in Austin, Texas, Matt Russell found: "Most people left church . . . because people in the church have the tendency to be small and mean and couldn't deal honestly with their own sins or the sin of others. As one man put it, 'People in the church were more invested in the process of being right than in the process of being honest [a little Be Like Me action].'"[12]

Skye Jethani of *Christianity Today* added her thoughts to Russell's research. "Russell spent a lot of time with de-churched people in recovery from drugs, alcohol, sex addiction, eating disorders, and gambling. The level of healing and transformation many of them experienced in their recovery groups was far greater than what they ever knew in the church. . . . [They are part of a larger group of] deeply committed Christians who are finding more meaningful authenticity, mission, and transformation outside the institutional structures of the church."[13]

In light of these observations, I want to expand on our roles, as we Christians gather and support one other:

- Churches should be places where we see each other's human misbehavior and unconditionally love and accept one another,

11. Ibid., 48–50, 54–55.
12. Jethani, Skye, "Who are the De-Churched?"
13. Ibid.

> while seeking healing for our imperfections. It should be a safe place for us to share what is really going on in our lives.
>
> - Christians should also help one another deal with our human misbehavior. I don't think we fulfill that role well. We identify some "obvious" misbehavior of others while hiding our own "less obvious" ones. Many of the misbehaviors (games) in this book are not faced and dealt with among Christians. We are not really transparent about our own "stuff."

That is my reason for writing this book and hopefully your reason for reading it—to help us (whether Christian or not) be more authentic and transparent with each other, identifying the misbehaviors we tend to hide in our relationship games. Then we can deal with these games, and we can help each other change to be more loving.

13

Living Authentically with God

I GET IT. God wants to reconcile our relationships—to him and to each other. And his spirit is in me, empowering me. He really is the ultimate game changer. This is not just a one-time event. It's an ongoing process, and for me it's not a process of continuous improvement. It's also not two steps forward and one step back—even that is too straightforward. Instead, I feel like I wander through my relationship with God (kind of like I wander through my relationships with other people).

I hear Beth talk about her desire for God, her intimate times with him in prayer, and God speaking to her as she spends time with him. I am glad for her, and at the same time I am jealous of her—her ability to relate to God like this. It makes me want to protect myself and play some games:

- I want to use my ESP to play a Don't Change Me Game. Of course, Beth's love language is quality time. So her personality leads her to relate to God this way. That's not me, not how God made me.

- Or Beth is such an extrovert that she easily shares with God what's going on in her heart and life. That's not me, either. God made me an introvert.

- It feels like I'm just being defensive in a Don't Change Me or Avoiding Responsibility Game, using my personality as an excuse for not having an open, honest relationship with the personal life-giver of the universe.

HOW DO I TRY TO PLAY GAMES WITH GOD?

Am I playing games with God like I do with others? You know, I see other people playing games with God, so if I recognize them playing games with God, I bet I must be doing it, too. Probably I'm playing some of the same games I see them playing, just in a different way. So what games do I think other people play with God? That may help me identify my own games. How about a couple of obvious ones, ones I have identified (judged) as hypocritical in the past:

- I see people playing Isolation Games with God, where they withdraw from him until they need him. God is their backup Plan B, if their Plan A doesn't work. Then they start playing Serve Me Games, asking God to help them, especially if they act right. I think I have moved beyond some of this gamesmanship. I don't expect to earn God's favor, because I'm already confident that he loves me. On the other hand, I recently was headed to a client meeting and on this occasion I was talking to God as I was driving. I remember telling God, "I feel pretty good about this meeting. I'm okay handling this one on my own. You can go help someone else." As soon as I said it, I realized how arrogant that was. God was going to be my fallback Plan B if my Plan A fell apart, and in this case Plan A was looking pretty good. The sad thing is I didn't even think about seeking God's power to make me more loving, more authentic as I dealt with this client—it was all about the meeting being successful from a business point of view.

- I see people playing Looking Good Games with God, where they show up at church to act righteous, but they will cheat on their wives or deceive their customers. I like to think I am not judging them, just stating the facts. I try to resist gossiping about them (out loud anyway). I somehow justify my actions by praying for them, too (when I think about it). I also act like them by trying to play a One-Sided Win-Win Game with God. I do just enough "righteous" service for God, so that I can rationalize doing some things I want to do, too. I must think that he has this chart where he tracks my good deeds (the ones I did when I didn't want to do them—they get extra credit). He compares those against my selfish deeds (the ones I did, when I really didn't think he wanted me to do them).

When I think about it, playing games with God seems so fruitless, so silly. How do I think these games can really protect me from the all-knowing and all-powerful God? Even more ironic, why do I feel the need to protect myself from the personal God who loves me enough to give his life for me? Maybe this is it. In spite of all he has done and said, I must not actually trust him. He seems so "inconsistent, so maddeningly unpredictable. One set of parents raises an honor student, a youth leader. Another set, equally good, maybe even better, places their son in drug rehab. One man's ministry takes off. . . . Another man, just as godly, watches his ministry die. Why?"[1]

I naturally want a God-formula, not a relationship with God. You know, if I do this, God does that. I want a God-formula that I can rely on. I'm afraid to trust in the uncertainties of a relationship. I want to read the Bible, pull out the consistent principles for successful living, live my life by those principles, and at the end say, "I lived and loved according to God's formula and I did the best I could—what a successful life!" I wonder what God will give me on my end-of-life performance appraisal—maybe a 7 or even an 8. Hopefully not a 2 or a 3. (Not much relationship needed with this formula approach. Relationships are so messy anyway.)

I want to find other formulas to live by, too. To live authentically, it would be really helpful to have a book about the relationship games we all play. Maybe that book would show me how I protect myself with these games. Then it would help me recognize those games and offer me some game changers to transform me so I actually live and love authentically. I would like to turn all those insightful ideas into formulas to ensure my life worked. (I hear there's a book in process on that very topic. I wonder if the book will give me formulas that ensure authentic success.)

Here's the problem. From the way I read how Jesus revealed God in the New Testament (kind of like the New Deal in our relationships), God is not a formula and the Bible is more than a "road map . . . [more than] a wordy version of MapQuest."[2] God has revealed himself as a person, not a list of Dos and Don'ts. As Donald Miller says, if God were a God of formulas, he would have written the Bible like a PowerPoint presentation—godly principles outlined with bullet points. But the Bible is a book of stories about God and people relating to each other, revealing the truth about God and life in the midst of their relationships. Even Jesus' instructions are often told in stories, where one's attitude is the key issue.[3] The Dos and Don'ts from Jesus illustrate how we are to love God

---

1. Crabb, *Shattered Dreams*, 48.
2. Presson, *When Will My Life*, 9.
3. Miller, *Searching*, 151–157.

and love others—they certainly aren't exhaustive and they aren't all perfectly clear. What is clear is that God has taken all the steps to reconcile us to himself through Christ, because we could never be good enough.

So why do I keep trying to negotiate the Deal? Why do I keep playing these games, not just with others, but even with God? In my natural self, I don't want to give up ultimate control over my life, over how I live. I want to figure him out and put him in a predictable box. If I know the rules, I can obey them like teenagers often obey the family rules, manipulating the rules more than they obey them. That's how I am tempted to work out my life with God, too. Obey the letter of the law without obeying the spirit of the law—isn't that enough? That's when I start playing games, trying to manipulate God like I try to manipulate other people. Looking like I'm obedient and loving, while still looking out for myself.

I want to define God in my predictable box, and he wants a trusting relationship. I want to give him good behavior, and God wants my heart. No wonder it's so hard—I want to protect my heart. I want some measure of safety in an unsafe world, and I still think the key to being safe is protecting myself. As C. S. Lewis says through one of his characters, Aslan [God] "isn't safe but he's good."[4] I keep looking for safe. I want a reliable formula. Too often I refuse to fling myself into our good God's arms and get ready for the ride of my life. It's still so hard for me to trust God with the outcome.

HOW CAN I TRUST GOD ENOUGH TO LIVE AUTHENTICALLY WITH HIM?

What game changer would convince me to trust God with the outcome? I have to know he loves me, that he has my best interest in mind. Paul encouraged the believers in Rome by writing to them that "God causes all things to work together for good to those who love God, to those who are called according to his purpose" (Rom 8:28). As a friend says, "I just don't know how bad God's best for me is going to get."

Since God is love, Jan Johnson suggests that we can better understand and experience God's love by replacing "love" with "God" in the New Testament vision of love (1 Cor 13: 4–8a)[5]:

---

4. Lewis, *The Lion*, 76.
5. Johnson, *Invitation*, 115–116.

- God is patient and kind.
- God is not jealous or boastful.
- God is not proud.
- God is not rude or self-seeking.
- He is not easily angered nor does he keep a record of wrongs.
- God does not delight in evil but he rejoices with the truth.
- He always protects, always trusts, always hopes, always perseveres.
- God never fails.[6]

Obviously there is more to an infinite God than this, but Johnson is right. Knowing I am loved this way by God is comforting, reassuring, even freeing. I'm free to actually trust him.

So if I do trust God and his love for me, if I stop trying to control my life, what does an authentic relationship with God look like? Funny thing, I think we already covered this topic in chapter 9. There we envisioned what an authentic relationship with other people looks like. Maybe an authentic relationship with God looks similar, something like this:

- Empathetic with God—I will be eager to know, experience, love, and serve God. He loves and even serves me, so I just return back to him his love and service. Wow! Another thought—can I really empathize with God? Can I choose to see things the way God sees them? I want to listen to him. That will be transforming!

- Transparent with God—I will want to talk to God. I want to be honest and loving and transparent as I share myself with God. I will not hold anything back, knowing he loves and accepts me no matter what I'm thinking or feeling or doing. I will rest in his redemption of my actions, emotions, and even my attitudes.

- Self-awareness through God's eyes--I want to understand more about myself, especially what God's perspective is on my passions and my dreams, my apparent successes and my perceived failures. What really drives my thoughts? How can I be the new creation God has invited me to be—remade, reconciled, and renewed?

- Letting go to God—In the end, I want to trust God with the outcome. I want to trust that he is using all aspects of my life to

---

6. Morris, *1 Corinthians*, 180–182.

draw me to want the greatest desire—the dream of experiencing him above all else. You know, we talk about loving other people unconditionally. When I let go of the outcome, I am loving God unconditionally. I am loving God without any expectations of him making my life easier—no conditions, just trust.

Yes! I want to live this life with God! I commit to live this life with you, God!

> **INTERPRETING AND APPLYING THE BIBLE THROUGH RELATIONSHIPS**
>
> It seems obvious to me that God reveals himself and his truth in biblical accounts of relationships. Even the truths in the New Deal are primarily told in Jesus' biographies, early church history, and letters—you can't find a more relationship-centered approach than this one. God also seems to reveal his truth for our lives in a manner that requires us to talk about how to interpret and apply what he says. It seems to me that is the reason his Dos and Don'ts aren't always clear on what they mean in any specific situation. We need a relationship with God and with each other to discuss what God is saying and how it applies to me today.
>
> Some people are turned off by this lack of clarity from the Bible and just give up. Others want to match up different passages from the Bible to come up with the one true interpretation and convince us they are right in their PowerPoint summary of biblical truth. Instead of following either of these approaches, I want to take advantage of this apparent gift from God and use this lack of clarity as an opportunity to dialogue about how each of us interprets and applies the Bible to our lives—another opportunity for an authentic relationship. We can even use it as an opportunity to interact with God on the same issue—how would he have us apply his truth to this specific situation? We can share our stories of how God is working through these situations as we wrestle with God's word to us.
>
> What an idea! As you and I share what God is teaching us through a passage from the Bible, we can better understand how to live according to God's word. Our conversations and our relationships help complete God's word in each of us as he works in our lives.

14

Where Are You, God?

So what's going on when our best attempts to reconcile and love each other don't work out? I want to live this authentic relationship with God and others, but you and I both mess it up. Where is God's power? Where is the new creation?

I have been depressed about this type of issue this week. We are part of a group with a passion for the same goal. No one disagrees about our overall objectives. Yet this week a couple of the leaders had a major disagreement about how to handle an issue. It appeared one person had not followed through on his commitment, which jeopardized our mission. Another person felt judged. A few e-mails flew around that added fuel to the fire. Looking back on it, several of us were speculating motives with ESP Games, wishing others were like us (playing both active and passive Be Like Me Games), and not really disclosing what we were really thinking or feeling (playing Isolation and Looking Good Games).

After the issue escalated, we did many of the "right things." I'm confident we all prayed for God to intervene in the situation. Two people met separately first and reconciled some misunderstandings. Then we met as a group and uncovered some other miscommunications, which cleared up more reasons behind the hurt feelings. A couple of people apologized for their roles in the issue. Even after all that work, one person felt "okay" that most of the issues had been resolved, and another one was still concerned that "he won't look me in the eye." We all affirmed our commitment and passion for the group's goals. The best answer left was, "Well, we just need to give it some time" for the healing process to continue working.

As I think about the loving solutions to our games, we could have done a better job disclosing our fears and intentions and feelings during the group meeting. While we listened to each other and did apologize for some of our actions, I don't recall using reflective listening to clarify what someone else was saying or feeling. We mainly were clearing up all the miscommunication on a logical plain, which had probably been fed by the ESP Games we were all playing. (It's sad, but I didn't even think about reviewing these loving solutions before our dinner. I just followed along, trying to work on reaching an agreement on the next steps, not trying to empathize or be transparent. I'm frustrated with myself. I wrote the book [literally], and I didn't even follow my own recommendations to authentically and lovingly work through this situation.)

So where are you, God? Or the better question may be, "Where are we, God?" We are a group of believers committed to knowing and loving God and each other. We obviously have not read and agreed on the suggestions in this book at this point, but we know enough to apply some of these loving solutions. Hey, Beth and I actually knew about everything in this book. We have your Holy Spirit. We are your new creation. I believe we all prayed for God's power to heal this situation, to reconcile us to one another.

Don't get me wrong—it could have been a lot worse. However, I look at the group and I feel helpless and even hopeless that two of these people will ever really understand and accept each other. I think they will each continue to be skeptical of each other. God, aren't you here in us? If we can't fully reconcile with all our knowledge of our games and these game changers plus your power in our lives, what's the use of trying?

Yes, this is depressing.

- Maybe my standards are too high for a fallen world. I certainly don't meet these high standards in my own life.
- Or maybe I'm too impatient. Maybe God still has more work to do in each of us in the group, not just these two people, and I would rather be moving onto greater (and easier) things.
- Maybe I'm trying to avoid whatever God is trying to teach me in all this, by concentrating on the apparent conflict of these two people. I just don't know.

I remember that Paul promised the Romans that "in all things God works for the good of those who love him" (Romans 8:28 NIV). Ruth

Myers apparently remembered that promise too, when she journaled this prayer to God:

> Thank you, my loving and sovereign Lord, that my failures and mistakes are part of the "all things" you work together for good . . . as well as my tensions and stresses, my hostile and anxious feelings, my regrets, my trips into shame and self-blame—and the specific things that trigger them. [It sounds like Myers had read about my frustrations with my friends and me in this chapter.] I praise you that "all things," including these, can contribute to my spiritual growth and my experience of you. . . .
>
> I rejoice that these things keep reminding me to depend on you with all my heart . . . that they prompt me to trust in your love. Your forgiveness. Your power. Your sufficiency. Your ability to overrule, and your transforming presence within me. . . . I praise you for . . . amazing grace, that enables me to hold my head high, not in pride but in humble gratitude for your undeserved, unchanging love, and total cleansing.[1]

So where else do I go, except to trust you, God, even when it doesn't look like I can trust you, or trust other people, or even trust myself? I'm back to my only workable choice—let go of the outcome and try to love and live authentically, even when the results don't match my expectations. Just keep trusting in your transforming presence within me. I am reminded of Josiah Bancroft's reflections on a similar conflict with his landlord and with his wife, Barbara:

> What counts is faith working through love, faith expressing itself in the way I love Barbara and the way we love our landlord. . . . And when I . . . make smaller things my focus, like my reputation, like worrying about what the landlord thinks about me . . . guess what's flowing out—demand, pressure, requirements . . . ?
>
> What is the answer for that? . . . I need to believe the Holy Spirit will use me [and] . . . God loves me even when I struggle like this. I need to believe God loves my wife and he's called me to love her and that loving her is really what's important. And that God has called us both to love my landlord as best we're able and to work for his good. . . .
>
> [God] keeps saying things back to me like, "The Holy Spirit is in your life. You haven't been left alone. . . . You could ask me to work in your heart, your wife's heart, and your landlord's heart, and I will. . . . Will you trust me in this situation? If you don't

---

1. Myers, *31 Days*, 94–95.

know what to do, if you'll wait, if you'll believe, if you'll rest in my spirit, I will lead you. I will step in and show you how best to love. And maybe you'll do that perfectly and maybe you won't. But I'll be with you and I will help you through it."[2]

In the midst of the reality of our interactions with one another, both what appears to be good and what appears to be bad, this is where I want to be. I want to rest in knowing God is with me, accepting me, guiding me in our joint quest to reconcile and redeem our relationships.

That's the purpose of this book—fulfilling that joint quest to redeem our relationships by:

- exposing eight games that cripple our relationships;
- examining the self-protective motives that lead us to play these games (from passively playing it safe to actively manipulating others to serve us);
- exploring some game changers—loving solutions to replace our games;
- envisioning a lifestyle of authentic living—self-aware, transparent, empathetic, and letting go of the outcome;
- encountering God as the ultimate game changer.

Our games are real, and they mess us up. These loving solutions are helpful, but they are not perfect. (Even if they were perfect, we're not perfect.) God's power is overwhelmingly able to change us into the new creation we were meant to be, and yet he lets us choose whether to yield to that power.

Lord, keep working in my life and in the lives of others! I can't wait to see where you take us, whether in comfort or pain. Grow us. Please transform us! Stop our self-protective games, sink our self-focused lifeboat, and set us free to be authentic lovers!

---

2. Bancroft, *Sonship*, Lecture 8.

Bibliography

A. A. World Services, Inc. "The Twelve Steps of Alcoholics Anonymous." No pages. Rev. May 9, 2002. Online: http://www.aa.org/en_pdfs/smf-121_en.pdf.

Bancroft, Josiah. *Sonship Lecture 8*. World Harvest Mission Sonship Lectures. Greensboro, NC: New Growth Press, 2002. CD set.

Bell, Rob. *Velvet Elvis: Repainting the Christian Faith*. Grand Rapids: Zondervan, 2005.

Berne, Eric. *Games People Play: The Psychology of Human Relationships*. 1964. Reprint, New York: Ballantine Books, 2004.

Chapman, Gary. *Building Relationships: A Discipleship Program for Married Couples*. Winston-Salem, NC: Marriage and Family Life Consultants, 1983.

———. *Love as a Way of Life: Seven Keys to Transforming Every Aspect of Your Life*. New York: Random House, 2009.

A Christmas Carol, directed by Clive Donner. Los Angeles: Twentieth Century Fox, 1984. DVD, 100 minutes.

Crabb, Larry. *The Pressure's Off: There's a New Way to Live*. Colorado Springs: Waterbrook Press, 2002.

———. *Real Church: Does It Exist? Can I Find It?* Nashville: Thomas Nelson, 2009.

———. *Shattered Dreams: God's Unexpected Pathway to Joy*. Colorado Springs: Waterbrook Press, 2001.

———. *Soul Talk: The Language God Longs for Us to Speak*. Nashville: Integrity Publishers, 2003.

"Edward Kennedy Memorial Service—VP Joe Biden Part 1," YouTube video, 10:36, from the August 28, 2009, memorial service at the JFK Presidential Library in Boston, uploaded by PoliticsNewsPolitics on August 28, 2009, http://www.youtube.com/watch?v=03jzJkSxLjU.

Edwards, Dwight. *Revolution Within: A Fresh Look at Supernatural Living*. Colorado Springs: Waterbrook Press, 2001.

Eldredge, John. *Wild at Heart: Discovering the Secret of a Man's Soul*. Nashville: Thomas Nelson, 2001.

Falcon, Ted and David Blatner. *Judaism for Dummies*. New York: Hungry Minds, 2001.

Foster, Richard J. *Celebration of Discipline: The Path to Spiritual Growth*. New York: HarperCollins, 1998.

"Good Luck Bad Luck!" No Pages. Online: http://www.naute.com/inspiration/luck.phtml.

Jethani, Skye, "Who are the De-Churched? (Part 1)." No pages. Article published March 16, 2010. Online: http://www.outofur.com/archives/2010/03/who_are_the_dec.html.

Johnson, Jan. *Invitation to the Jesus Life: Experiments in Christlikeness*. Colorado Springs: NavPress, 2008.

Bibliography

Kinnaman, David and Gabe Lyons. *UnChristian: What a New Generation Really Thinks About Christianity*. Grand Rapids: Baker Books, 2007.

Lewis, C. S. *The Lion, the Witch, and the Wardrobe*. New York: Collier Books, 1970.

Lineberry, Joe and Beth Lineberry. *"Give Me Your Son" and Other Reflections from our Journey*. Winston-Salem, NC: Possibilities, 2008.

Manning, Brennan. *Souvenirs of Solitude: Finding Rest in Abba's Embrace*. Colorado Springs: NavPress, 2009.

Miller, Donald. *Searching for God Knows What*. Nashville: Thomas Nelson, 2004.

Moore, Beth. "If You Remain Silent." Session four, disc three. *Esther: It's Tough Being a Woman*. Nashville: Lifeway Press, 2008. DVD set.

Morris, Leon. *1 Corinthians*. Tyndale New Testament Commentaries, rev. ed. 1985. Reprint, Grand Rapids: William B. Eerdmans, 1996.

Myers, Ruth. *31 Days of Praise: Enjoying God Anew*. Colorado Springs: Multnomah Books, 1994.

Presson, Ramon. *When Will My Life Not Suck?: Authentic Hope for the Disillusioned*. Greensboro, NC: New Growth Press, 2011.

Smith, Melinda, et al., "Laughter is the Best Medicine: The Health Benefits of Humor and Laughter." No pages. Rev. May 2010. Online: http://helpguide.org/life/humor_laughter_health.htm.

Ward, Deborah, "Passive-Aggressive Personality: Characteristics of Negativistic Personality Disorder." No pages. Article published November 14, 2008. Online: http://personalitydisorders.suite101.com/article.cfm/passiveaggressive_personality#ixzz0GZ62PSX6&A.

Willard, Dallas. *The Divine Conspiracy: Rediscovering Our Hidden Life in God*. New York: HarperCollins, 1997.

Young, William P. *The Shack: Where Tragedy Confronts Eternity*. Los Angeles: Windblown Media, 2007.

Zacharias, Karen Spears. *Where's Your Jesus Now?: Examining How Fear Erodes our Faith*. Grand Rapids: Zondervan, 2008.

www.ingramcontent.com/pod-product-compliance
Lightning Source LLC
Chambersburg PA
CBHW051932160426
43198CB00012B/2117